Dedication

This book is dedicated to all the entrepreneurs, small business owners, and marketing professionals who tirelessly work to build their online presence. It's for those who believe in the power of organic growth, sustainable strategies, and the long-term value of building genuine connections with their audience. This book is a testament to your dedication, resilience, and unwavering commitment to success in the ever-evolving digital landscape. It's a guide to navigate the complexities of online marketing, offering practical tools and proven strategies to help you achieve your business goals. To those who face challenges head-on, who learn from their mistakes, and who never stop striving for improvement – this book is for you. Your perseverance inspires us all. May this guide serve as a valuable resource to help you reach your full potential and achieve the online success you deserve. This is dedicated to the dreamers, the doers, and the believers – those who dare to imagine a brighter future and work relentlessly to make it a reality. May this book empower you to build an impactful online presence that reflects your hard work, passion, and commitment.

Preface

In today's hyper-connected world, a strong online presence isn't just a luxury; it's a necessity for businesses of all sizes. However, the digital marketing landscape can often feel overwhelming, filled with conflicting advice, fleeting trends, and the constant pressure to "go viral." This book, "Get Seen Online," offers a refreshing alternative: a practical, step-by-step guide to building a sustainable and effective online strategy without chasing viral fame. We've distilled years of experience in digital marketing and strategy into a concise, actionable resource, designed to equip you with the knowledge and tools needed to succeed. Forget the hype and the fleeting trends; focus on building a solid foundation based on proven principles and strategies. Within these pages, you'll discover how to optimize your website for search engines, leverage the power of social media without sacrificing authenticity, build a loyal email list, and create engaging content that resonates with your target audience. This isn't a theoretical guide; it's a hands-on manual filled with real-world examples, case studies, and practical checklists to help you implement each strategy effectively. Whether you're a seasoned marketing professional or a small business owner just starting out, this book provides the roadmap to a thriving online presence. Let's embark on this journey together – let's get you seen online.

Introduction

The digital age presents unparalleled opportunities for businesses to connect with their target audience, build brand awareness, and drive sales. However, navigating the complexities of online marketing can be daunting. Many businesses fall into the trap of chasing fleeting viral trends, investing time and resources in strategies that yield short-term gains but lack long-term sustainability. "Get Seen Online" provides a practical alternative – a proven approach to building a strong and sustainable online presence focused on organic growth and lasting results. This book is designed to be your comprehensive guide to effective online marketing, demystifying the complexities and providing you with actionable strategies you can implement immediately. We will explore a range of crucial topics, including search engine optimization (SEO), social media marketing, email marketing, paid advertising, and content marketing. Through real-world examples and insightful case studies, we'll illustrate how to effectively use these channels to reach your target audience, build a loyal following, and achieve your business objectives. We'll emphasize the importance of understanding your audience deeply, setting realistic goals, and consistently measuring your results. This book isn't about quick fixes or get-rich-quick schemes; it's about building a solid foundation for long-term online success. Prepare to learn how to create a digital strategy that resonates with your audience, builds trust, and drives sustainable growth for years to come. Let's begin building your lasting online presence.

Defining Your Target Audience and Their Online Behavior

Before you can effectively reach your audience online, you need to understand who they are and how they behave in the digital world. This isn't about generic assumptions; it's about creating a detailed profile of your ideal customer, a process that goes beyond simple demographics. We'll delve into the crucial techniques of audience profiling, ensuring you grasp the nuances of their online habits and preferences. This understanding forms the bedrock of any successful online marketing strategy. Without it, your efforts risk being scattered and ineffective, like shouting into a crowded room without knowing who you're trying to reach.

The first step is identifying your ideal customer profile (ICP). This involves moving beyond basic demographics like age, gender, and location. While this information is helpful, it only scratches the surface. To truly understand your audience, you need to explore their psychographics—their values, interests, lifestyle, attitudes, and opinions. Consider what motivates them, what problems they face, and what solutions they seek. For example, a company selling organic skincare products would target a very different audience than a company selling high-end gaming PCs. The organic skincare company might focus on environmentally conscious individuals concerned with health and wellness, while the gaming PC company targets tech-savvy individuals who prioritize performance and immersion.

To effectively define your target audience, ask yourself crucial questions: What are their pain points? What are their aspirations? What are their online habits? What kind of content do they consume? Where do they spend most of their time online (Facebook, Instagram, TikTok, LinkedIn, niche forums, etc.)? What devices do they use to access the internet (desktop, mobile, tablet)? Are they active on social media? If so, which platforms? Do they engage with influencers? What are their preferred methods of communication (email, social media messaging, etc.)? What kind of content resonates most with them (informational, entertaining, inspirational)? What are their purchasing habits and decision-making processes? Do they tend to research extensively before making a purchase, or are they more impulsive buyers?

Once you've thoroughly answered these questions, you can start to create detailed buyer personas. These are semi-fictional representations of your ideal customers, based on your research and insights. Each persona should have a name, a detailed description of their demographics and psychographics, and a clear picture of their online behavior. Creating multiple personas might be necessary if your target audience is diverse. For example, a B2B SaaS company might have separate personas for marketing managers, CEOs, and IT directors. Each will have different needs, priorities, and online habits.

To gather data for your audience profiling, you can utilize a variety of tools and techniques:

Surveys and questionnaires: These are effective ways to directly collect information from your target audience. Use platforms like SurveyMonkey or Google Forms to create and distribute surveys. Keep them concise and focused to maximize response rates.

Social media listening: Monitor social media conversations related to your industry and target audience. Use tools like Brand24 or Mention to track mentions of your brand, competitors, and relevant keywords. This will provide valuable insights into their preferences and concerns.

Google Analytics: If you have a website, Google Analytics is an invaluable tool for understanding your website traffic and user behavior. You can see demographics, geographic locations, interests, and more.

Social media analytics: Most social media platforms provide built-in analytics tools that offer valuable data about your audience. Analyze the demographics, interests, engagement rates, and more to refine your understanding.

Customer Relationship Management (CRM) data: If you already have a CRM system, it's a goldmine of customer data. Analyze your customer data to identify patterns and trends in their demographics, purchasing habits, and preferences.

Focus groups and interviews: Conduct focus groups or individual interviews to gather qualitative data about your target audience's needs, motivations, and challenges. This provides deeper insight beyond quantitative data.

Let's consider a hypothetical example: A small local bakery wants to expand its online presence. Their demographic analysis might reveal their primary customers are women aged 25-55 with children. However, their psychographic analysis is crucial for effective marketing. Are they primarily interested in convenience, healthier options, supporting local businesses, or indulging in treats? Their online behavior will guide the marketing channels. Do they primarily use Facebook, Instagram, or perhaps participate in local community forums? Do they respond to influencer marketing? If they prefer Instagram, the bakery should focus its efforts on visually appealing content showcasing its baked goods. If local forums are more important, community engagement and partnerships are key. A clear understanding of their online behavior dictates where and how marketing efforts should be directed.

Another example: A tech startup developing a project management tool will need to analyze its target audience differently. Its demographics might include professionals aged 25-45 in various industries. Psychographically, they're likely driven by efficiency, productivity, and streamlining workflows. Their online behavior would likely involve LinkedIn, professional blogs, and industry-specific websites. Their engagement might be influenced by thought leadership content, webinars, or case studies demonstrating the software's effectiveness. The marketing strategy would reflect these insights, with a focus on professional networking and content marketing showcasing practical applications and ROI.

Understanding your audience's online behavior isn't a one-time task; it's an ongoing process. Regularly review your data and adapt your strategies as needed. The online landscape is constantly evolving, and your audience's preferences and habits will change over time. Continuous monitoring ensures your marketing efforts remain relevant and effective.

By investing time and effort in thoroughly understanding your target audience and their online behavior, you lay the foundation for a successful online marketing strategy that yields tangible results. This detailed knowledge guides your content creation, channel selection, and messaging, ensuring your efforts connect with the right people at the right time, increasing your chances of achieving your business objectives. It's the difference between shouting into the void and having a meaningful conversation with those who truly matter.

Setting Realistic Goals and Key Performance Indicators KPIs

Now that you have a deep understanding of your target audience, it's time to translate that knowledge into actionable strategies. This involves setting realistic goals and identifying key performance indicators (KPIs) to measure your progress. Without clear objectives and measurable metrics, your online marketing efforts will lack direction and you'll struggle to assess their effectiveness. This section guides you through the process of setting SMART goals and choosing relevant KPIs that directly contribute to your business objectives.

The first step is to define SMART goals. SMART stands for Specific, Measurable, Achievable, Relevant, and Time-bound. Let's break down each component:

Specific: Your goals should be clearly defined and leave no room for ambiguity. Avoid vague statements like "increase brand awareness." Instead, aim for something like "increase brand awareness by 20% among our target demographic on Instagram within the next quarter." The more specific your goal, the easier it is to measure progress and make necessary adjustments.

Measurable: Include quantifiable metrics in your goals so you can track your progress accurately. Instead of "improve website engagement," aim for "increase website bounce rate by 15% and average session duration by 20% within three months." This ensures you have concrete data to assess performance.

Achievable: While ambitious goals are important, they should also be realistic and attainable within a given timeframe. Setting unrealistic goals can lead to discouragement and demotivation. Consider your resources, budget, and existing capabilities when setting goals. Start with smaller, achievable goals and gradually increase the ambition as you gain momentum and experience.

Relevant: Your goals should be directly aligned with your overall business objectives. Focus on goals that contribute to your company's bottom line, whether it's increasing sales, generating leads, or building brand awareness. Avoid setting goals that are irrelevant to your business strategy.

Time-bound: Set a specific timeframe for achieving your goals. This creates a sense of urgency and helps you stay focused. Instead of "increase email subscribers," aim for "increase email subscribers by 500 within the next six months." Deadlines are essential for effective project management and monitoring progress.

Let's illustrate this with some examples:

Goal: Increase website traffic from organic search by 30% within the next six months. This is a SMART goal because it is specific (organic search traffic), measurable (30% increase), achievable (depending on your current traffic and SEO strategy), relevant (increases website visibility), and time-bound (six months).

Goal: Generate 100 qualified leads through a new social media campaign on LinkedIn within the next three months. This goal is specific (qualified leads from LinkedIn), measurable (100 leads), achievable (depending on your campaign strategy and target audience), relevant (generates sales opportunities), and time-bound (three months).

Goal: Improve customer satisfaction by 10% as measured by customer surveys within the next year. This goal is specific (customer satisfaction), measurable (10% improvement), achievable (depending on your customer service efforts), relevant (improves brand loyalty and reputation), and time-bound (one year).

Once you have established SMART goals, the next step is to define key performance indicators (KPIs). KPIs are specific metrics that help you track progress towards your goals. Choosing the right KPIs is crucial for monitoring your online marketing effectiveness and identifying areas for improvement.

Here are some common KPIs for online marketing:

Website Traffic: This measures the number of visitors to your website. You can track this using Google Analytics and examine metrics like unique visitors, page views, bounce rate, and average session duration. A high bounce rate suggests problems with website usability or content relevance. Low average session duration might indicate a lack of engaging content.

Lead Generation: This tracks the number of potential customers who have shown interest in your products or services. Key metrics include the number of form submissions, email sign-ups, and demo requests. Analyzing the sources of your leads (organic search, social media, paid advertising) can help optimize your marketing efforts.

Conversion Rates: This measures the percentage of visitors who complete a desired action, such as making a purchase, signing up for a newsletter, or filling out a contact form. Monitoring conversion rates helps identify bottlenecks in your sales funnel and improve your website's effectiveness in converting visitors into customers.

Social Media Engagement: This measures how users interact with your social media content. Metrics include likes, comments, shares, retweets, and mentions. High engagement suggests your content resonates with your audience and your social media strategy is effective. Low engagement may indicate a need to refine your content strategy or target audience.

Customer Acquisition Cost (CAC): This represents the total cost of acquiring a new customer. It helps assess the efficiency of your marketing efforts and identify cost-effective strategies.

Return on Investment (ROI): This measures the profitability of your marketing initiatives. It compares the cost of your marketing campaigns with the revenue generated. A high ROI indicates successful marketing strategies.

Email Marketing Metrics: Open rates, click-through rates, and conversion rates from email campaigns are crucial for measuring email marketing effectiveness. Analyzing these metrics helps optimize email content and targeting.

Brand Mentions: Tracking mentions of your brand across various online platforms provides insights into brand awareness and reputation. Positive mentions are favorable, while negative mentions might indicate areas for improvement in customer service or product quality.

To effectively monitor these KPIs, utilize various analytics tools:

Google Analytics: Provides comprehensive website traffic data, including demographics, geographic location, device usage, and user behavior. You can use this data to understand your website audience and optimize its content and structure.

Google Search Console: Provides information on your website's performance in Google search results, including keyword rankings, impressions, and click-through rates. This data helps optimize your SEO strategy and improve your website's visibility in search results.

Social Media Analytics: Most social media platforms offer built-in analytics dashboards, allowing you to track engagement, reach, and demographics for each post. This data helps understand which content resonates with your audience and optimize your social media strategies.

CRM Systems: CRM software stores customer data, providing insights into customer behavior, purchase history, and preferences. This information helps personalize marketing efforts and enhance customer relationships.

Establishing a baseline is crucial before you begin implementing your marketing strategies. This involves analyzing your current performance across your chosen KPIs. This data provides a benchmark against which you can compare future results, allowing you to accurately assess the effectiveness of your marketing initiatives. Without a baseline, it's impossible to gauge improvement or identify areas needing attention.

Setting incremental milestones is also essential for maintaining momentum and celebrating achievements. Break down your larger goals into smaller, more manageable milestones, setting realistic targets for each stage of the process. Achieving these smaller milestones provides motivation and reinforces progress, enhancing commitment and driving continued effort.

Remember, setting realistic goals and tracking KPIs is an iterative process. Regularly review your progress, analyze your data, and adjust your strategies as needed. The online landscape is dynamic; continuous monitoring and adaptation are key to success. By consistently tracking your KPIs and making data-driven decisions, you can ensure your online marketing efforts remain effective and contribute meaningfully to your business objectives.

Choosing the Right Online Marketing Channels

Now that you've established SMART goals and identified key performance indicators (KPIs), it's time to select the online marketing channels that will best help you achieve those goals. Choosing the right channels is paramount; spreading your resources too thinly across numerous platforms can be inefficient, while focusing solely on one or two might miss out on significant opportunities. This decision hinges heavily on your target audience, your business objectives, and your budget.

Let's delve into some of the most prevalent online marketing channels and analyze their strengths and weaknesses:

Search Engine Optimization (SEO): SEO focuses on improving your website's organic ranking in search engine results pages (SERPs). A high ranking means increased visibility to users searching for products or services related to your business. This is a long-term strategy; it takes time and effort to build up your organic ranking. However, the rewards are significant: organic traffic is generally highly targeted and often converts well.

Advantages: High conversion rates, cost-effective in the long run, builds brand credibility and trust.
Disadvantages: Time-consuming, requires ongoing effort and optimization, algorithms are constantly changing, results are not immediate.
Example: A local bakery could optimize its website for keywords like "best croissants near me," "bakery delivery," or "gluten-free bread." This would attract customers actively searching for those specific products in their area.

Social Media Marketing: Social media platforms provide avenues to connect directly with your target audience. By creating engaging content and running targeted advertising campaigns, you can build brand awareness, generate leads, and drive traffic to your website. The choice of platform depends heavily on your target demographic; for instance, LinkedIn is ideal for B2B marketing, while Instagram is better suited for visually-driven products.

Advantages: Direct connection with customers, ability to build community, cost-effective advertising options, versatile content formats.
Disadvantages: Requires consistent content creation, algorithms can fluctuate, organic reach can be limited, success depends on understanding each platform's nuances.
Example: A clothing brand could use Instagram to showcase its new collection through visually appealing photos and videos, engaging with followers through stories and live sessions, and running targeted ads to reach specific demographics based on interests, age, or location.

Email Marketing: Email remains a powerful tool for nurturing leads and building customer relationships. By collecting email addresses through website forms or contests, you can send targeted messages about new products, promotions, or relevant industry news. Effective email campaigns require a well-segmented list and compelling content.

Advantages: High conversion rates, allows for personalized messaging, relatively cost-effective, measurable results.
Disadvantages: Requires email list building, can be perceived as spam if not managed carefully, email deliverability can be affected by various factors, requires ongoing content creation.

Example: A software company could send regular newsletters to subscribers with updates on new features, tutorials, and industry insights. They could also segment their list to send targeted promotions to users based on their usage patterns or previous purchases.

Paid Advertising (PPC): Pay-per-click (PPC) advertising involves paying for your ads to appear at the top of search engine results or on social media feeds. This can generate instant traffic and leads, but requires careful management to ensure a positive return on investment. Keyword research, ad copywriting, and bid management are crucial elements for success.

Advantages: Quick results, targeted reach, measurable results, flexible budget allocation.
Disadvantages: Can be expensive, requires ongoing optimization, requires knowledge of platform-specific advertising policies, requires constant monitoring and adjustments to campaigns.
Example: A financial services company could run PPC ads on Google for keywords like "investment advice" or "retirement planning," targeting specific demographics and locations. They could also use social media PPC advertising to reach potential clients on platforms like Facebook and LinkedIn.

Content Marketing: Creating valuable, relevant, and consistent content attracts and engages a clearly defined audience – and, ultimately, drives profitable customer action. This encompasses blog posts, articles, videos, infographics, podcasts, and more. The goal is to establish your business as a thought leader and build trust with your audience.

Advantages: Builds brand authority, improves organic search ranking, attracts high-quality leads, establishes long-term relationships with customers.

Disadvantages: Time-consuming to create high-quality content, requires a consistent publishing schedule, results are not immediate, measuring the ROI can be challenging.

Example: A technology company could publish blog posts on industry trends, white papers on complex technical topics, and video tutorials on using their software. This would position them as experts and attract potential customers seeking information and solutions in their field.

Choosing the Right Mix: The ideal online marketing strategy rarely relies on a single channel. A balanced approach, tailored to your specific needs and resources, is usually most effective. Consider the following factors when selecting your channels:

Target Audience: Where does your audience spend their time online? Which platforms do they use regularly? Understanding your audience's online behavior is crucial in selecting the right channels.

Business Objectives: What are you trying to achieve with your online marketing efforts? Are you trying to increase brand awareness, generate leads, drive sales, or something else? Your objectives will influence your choice of channels.

Budget: How much are you willing to invest in online marketing? Some channels, such as PPC advertising, can be quite expensive, while others, such as SEO and content marketing, are more cost-effective in the long run.

Resources: Do you have the in-house expertise or resources to manage multiple channels effectively? If not, you might need to outsource some tasks or focus on fewer channels initially.

Starting small and focusing on a few key channels is often the best approach, particularly for smaller businesses with limited resources. As you gain experience and achieve success, you can gradually expand your reach to include more channels. Regularly analyzing your results and adjusting your strategy based on data-driven insights is essential for maintaining effectiveness and maximizing your return on investment. Remember, consistency and patience are key to long-term success in online marketing. Don't expect overnight miracles; building a strong online presence takes time and effort. But by diligently following the strategies outlined in this book, you can build a sustainable and effective online strategy that will help your business thrive in the long term. Continuous learning and adaptation are crucial in this ever-evolving digital landscape; staying updated on the latest trends and best practices will ensure you remain ahead of the curve. This involves staying informed about algorithm updates, emerging technologies, and changes in user behavior. Regularly attending industry events, reading relevant publications, and participating in online communities can provide valuable insights and keep you abreast of the latest developments.

Remember to track your results carefully. Use analytics tools like Google Analytics, social media analytics dashboards, and email marketing platforms to monitor key performance indicators (KPIs) and assess the effectiveness of your chosen channels. This data will inform your future decisions, allowing you to refine your strategy and optimize your spending for maximum impact. By consistently analyzing your data and making data-driven decisions, you can ensure your online marketing efforts remain effective and contribute meaningfully to your overall business objectives. Don't be afraid to experiment and try new things. The online marketing landscape is constantly evolving, and what works today might not work tomorrow. Experimentation and adaptation are vital to success in this dynamic environment. Embrace innovation and be willing to try new approaches to stay ahead of the curve and maintain a competitive edge. The ultimate goal is to create a synergistic blend of channels that reinforces your message, reaches your target audience effectively, and drives tangible results for your business.

Building a Strong Brand Identity Online

Building a cohesive and compelling online brand identity is crucial for standing out in the crowded digital landscape. It's more than just a logo; it's the sum total of your brand's personality, values, and message, consistently communicated across all your online platforms. Think of your brand identity as the foundation upon which you build your entire online presence. A strong brand identity fosters trust, loyalty, and recognition, ultimately driving business growth. Without a clearly defined brand, your online efforts become fragmented and ineffective, losing the opportunity to create a lasting impression on your target audience.

The first step in building a strong online brand identity is to define your brand's core values and mission. What makes your business unique? What problems do you solve for your customers? What is your brand's personality – is it playful, professional, sophisticated, or something else? Articulating these core elements forms the bedrock of your brand messaging. This clarity allows for consistent communication across all channels, avoiding conflicting messages that confuse your audience and dilute your brand's impact. Consider conducting internal workshops or surveys to gather input from your team, ensuring everyone understands and embodies the brand's core tenets.

Next, develop a clear brand voice. This refers to the tone and style of your written and spoken communication. Is your brand formal or informal? Humorous or serious? Empathetic or authoritative? Consistency in your brand voice is paramount. Imagine a clothing brand using a playful, informal tone on Instagram but a stiff, overly professional tone on its website. This jarring inconsistency would confuse customers and damage brand credibility. Establishing a style guide for writing, including tone, vocabulary, and grammar, is a vital step in maintaining brand voice consistency.

Visual consistency is equally important. Your logo, color palette, typography, and imagery should all work together to create a unified and memorable visual identity. Consider using a brand style guide to ensure consistent application of these elements across all online channels. This guide should include detailed specifications for logo usage, color codes, font choices, and image styles, helping maintain a cohesive brand aesthetic across all platforms. Inconsistent visual elements create a fragmented and unprofessional image, harming brand recognition and recall.

Brand storytelling is a powerful tool for building emotional connections with your audience. Instead of simply listing features and benefits, craft compelling narratives that showcase your brand's values, mission, and unique selling points. This could involve sharing the story of your company's founding, highlighting customer success stories, or showcasing the passion and dedication behind your products or services. Authentic storytelling fosters a deeper connection with your audience, building trust and loyalty. Consider using various content formats such as blog posts, videos, and infographics to tell your brand's story effectively.

Creating a unique brand personality goes beyond simple aesthetics. It involves infusing your brand with a distinct character that resonates with your target audience. Is your brand the quirky friend, the reliable expert, the innovative leader? This personality should be reflected in your content, tone of voice, and visual elements. A clear brand personality helps your business stand out from competitors, making it more memorable and engaging for customers. Analyze your competitors to identify gaps and opportunities to create a distinctive brand personality that resonates uniquely with your audience.

Maintaining consistency across all online channels is critical. Your website, social media profiles, email marketing campaigns, and paid advertising should all project the same brand message, voice, and visual identity. This requires meticulous planning and coordination across all teams involved in your online marketing efforts. Regular brand audits can help identify areas where consistency is lacking and guide necessary adjustments. These audits involve analyzing your online presence across all platforms, checking for inconsistencies in messaging, visual elements, and brand voice.

Let's examine some brands with strong online identities. Apple, for example, consistently projects an image of minimalist design, innovation, and user-friendliness across all its platforms. Their website, social media presence, and product packaging all reflect this cohesive brand identity. Similarly, Nike's brand identity revolves around athleticism, motivation, and empowerment, consistently conveyed through their powerful imagery, inspirational messaging, and athlete endorsements. These brands understand the power of a consistent brand identity and leverage it to build strong customer relationships and market dominance.

Conducting regular brand audits is essential for maintaining brand consistency. These audits should involve a thorough review of your online presence, including your website, social media profiles, email campaigns, and any other online channels. Look for inconsistencies in messaging, visual elements, and brand voice. Tools such as brand monitoring software can help automate this process and identify potential problems early on. Identify gaps or inconsistencies and address them immediately. Regular monitoring ensures that your brand message remains consistent and resonates effectively with your audience. A consistent brand message builds trust and recognition, which are essential elements of successful online marketing.

Finally, remember that building a strong online brand identity is an ongoing process. The digital landscape is constantly evolving, and your brand identity may need to adapt over time to reflect changes in your business, your target audience, or the broader market. Regularly review and update your brand guidelines to ensure they remain relevant and effective. Stay current with trends and best practices, adapting your brand strategy to maintain a competitive advantage. By continuously refining your brand identity and adapting to the changing digital landscape, you can build a lasting presence that resonates with your audience and fuels business growth. Your online brand identity is a living entity, requiring consistent nurturing and refinement to maintain its effectiveness and relevance. The investment in a strong, consistent brand identity is an investment in the long-term success and sustainability of your business.

Website Optimization for Search Engines SEO

Search engine optimization (SEO) is the cornerstone of any successful online strategy. It's about making your website discoverable to potential customers actively searching for products or services like yours. Unlike paid advertising, which requires continuous spending, SEO focuses on organic, or unpaid, traffic. This means attracting visitors through search engine results, rather than paying for clicks. While it takes time and effort, the rewards of consistent, high-quality SEO are substantial: increased visibility, higher conversion rates, and ultimately, greater revenue.

The process begins with meticulous keyword research. This involves identifying the terms and phrases people use when searching for businesses like yours. Tools like Google Keyword Planner, Ahrefs, SEMrush, and Moz Keyword Explorer can provide valuable insights into search volume, competition, and keyword relevance. Don't just focus on high-volume keywords; consider long-tail keywords—more specific phrases with lower competition but higher conversion potential. For example, instead of targeting the broad keyword "shoes," consider long-tail keywords like "women's running shoes size 8," "men's leather dress shoes," or "best hiking boots for rocky terrain." This level of specificity attracts highly targeted traffic, leading to more qualified leads and higher conversion rates.

Once you've identified your target keywords, it's time for on-page optimization. This involves optimizing individual web pages to rank higher for specific keywords. This includes optimizing title tags, meta descriptions, header tags (H1-H6), image alt text, and URL slugs. Each element plays a crucial role in telling search engines what your page is about. Your title tag, for instance, should accurately reflect the page's content and include your primary keyword. Meta descriptions, while not directly impacting rankings, are crucial for enticing users to click through from the SERPs. They should be concise, compelling, and contain relevant keywords.

Header tags (H1-H6) help structure your content and signal to search engines the page's hierarchy and key topics. Your H1 tag should usually contain your primary keyword, while subsequent header tags can incorporate related keywords and subtopics. Image alt text is essential for accessibility and SEO. It provides a textual description of images, allowing search engines to understand their context. Ensure your alt text accurately describes the image and includes relevant keywords where appropriate. Finally, your URL slugs should be clear, concise, and include your primary keyword. Avoid long, complicated URLs filled with numbers and gibberish; keep them short, descriptive, and keyword-rich.

Beyond on-page optimization, off-page optimization is equally vital. This involves building your website's authority and reputation through external signals. One of the most effective off-page techniques is link building. Earning high-quality backlinks from reputable websites signals to search engines that your website is trustworthy and authoritative. Focus on acquiring links from relevant websites within your industry. Guest blogging, outreach, and building relationships with other website owners are effective strategies for acquiring backlinks. Don't resort to black hat SEO tactics like buying links, as these can severely harm your website's ranking.

Another key aspect of off-page optimization is social media marketing. While social media signals don't directly impact rankings, they indirectly influence SEO by driving traffic, brand awareness, and engagement. A strong social media presence can improve your website's visibility and authority. Make sure your social media profiles are optimized with relevant keywords and link back to your website. Consistent and engaging content on social media will attract followers and generate traffic. However, remember that social media marketing is not a replacement for SEO, but a complementary strategy to enhance its effectiveness.

Technical SEO focuses on the technical aspects of your website that affect its search engine visibility. This includes site speed, mobile-friendliness, site structure, and XML sitemaps. A slow website can lead to high bounce rates and poor user experience, ultimately harming your rankings. Optimize your website's loading speed by compressing images, minimizing HTTP requests, and leveraging browser caching. Ensuring your website is mobile-friendly is crucial, as an increasing number of searches are conducted on mobile devices. Google's Mobile-First Indexing means that the mobile version of your website is primarily used for ranking purposes.

A well-structured website with clear navigation and internal linking is essential for both users and search engines. Internal linking involves linking different pages on your website to each other, helping search engines crawl and index your content effectively. An XML sitemap provides search engines with a list of all the pages on your website, making it easier for them to find and index your content. Submitting your sitemap to Google Search Console can improve your website's discoverability. Regularly monitoring your website's technical SEO health is crucial for maintaining its rankings and improving its visibility.

Let's examine some real-world examples of effective SEO strategies. Consider a local bakery wanting to attract customers. Through keyword research, they identify keywords like "best croissants [city name]," "local bakery [neighborhood]," and "artisan bread delivery [zip code]." Their on-page optimization includes incorporating these keywords into their website content, title tags, and meta descriptions. Their off-page strategy focuses on building local citations, listing their bakery on relevant directories, and engaging with customers on social media. Their technical SEO includes ensuring their website is mobile-friendly and loads quickly.

Another example is a software company launching a new product. Their SEO strategy focuses on long-tail keywords related to the product's features and benefits. They create high-quality blog posts and other content pieces that address customer questions and concerns. They build relationships with relevant industry influencers and earn backlinks from reputable technology websites. Their technical SEO involves ensuring their website is secure (HTTPS), has a well-structured sitemap, and is optimized for mobile devices.

In both examples, a comprehensive SEO strategy incorporating keyword research, on-page and off-page optimization, and technical SEO is crucial for success. SEO isn't a one-time effort but an ongoing process that requires consistent monitoring and adaptation. Regularly analyze your website's performance using tools like Google Analytics and Google Search Console to track your rankings, traffic, and other key metrics. Analyze the performance of your keywords and adjust your strategy accordingly. Stay updated on the latest SEO best practices and algorithm updates, adapting your strategy as needed to maintain a competitive advantage. Remember that a successful SEO strategy is an integral part of a broader digital marketing plan, working synergistically with other strategies to achieve your business goals.

The digital landscape is dynamic, with search engine algorithms constantly evolving. Therefore, consistent monitoring and adaptation are crucial for long-term SEO success. Regularly analyze website data using tools like Google Analytics and Google Search Console to understand website performance, identify areas for improvement, and measure the effectiveness of SEO efforts. These analytics tools provide valuable insights into user behavior, traffic sources, and keyword performance.

Leverage SEO tools to streamline the process. Tools such as SEMrush, Ahrefs, and Moz offer advanced features for keyword research, competitor analysis, rank tracking, and backlink analysis. These tools help automate many aspects of SEO, saving time and providing valuable data-driven insights. Use this data to refine your strategy, ensuring your efforts remain targeted and effective. By integrating these tools into your workflow, you can efficiently monitor your progress and adapt your strategy to stay ahead of the curve.

Finally, remember that SEO is a marathon, not a sprint. Building a strong online presence takes time and consistent effort. Don't expect overnight results; focus on implementing a sustainable SEO strategy that aligns with your business goals. By committing to a well-structured SEO plan, regularly monitoring its effectiveness, and adapting to the ever-changing digital environment, you'll cultivate a robust online presence that drives organic traffic, enhances brand awareness, and ultimately fuels business growth. The investment in sustainable SEO is an investment in the future success of your online business.

Keyword Research and Targeting

Keyword research is the bedrock of any successful SEO strategy. It's the process of identifying the words and phrases people type into search engines when looking for products or services like yours. Without this crucial first step, your efforts to optimize your website will be largely ineffective, akin to aiming an arrow without a target. Effective keyword research doesn't simply involve listing random terms related to your business; it's about understanding the nuances of search intent and finding the keywords that best align with your target audience and business goals.

Several powerful tools can significantly simplify this process. Google Keyword Planner, a free tool integrated into Google Ads, is an excellent starting point. It provides insights into search volume, competition, and related keywords. However, its data is somewhat limited, providing only broad keyword suggestions. For more comprehensive data, consider investing in premium tools like Ahrefs, SEMrush, or Moz Keyword Explorer. These platforms offer more in-depth keyword analysis, including search volume, keyword difficulty, click-through rates, and competitive analysis. They also often provide long-tail keyword suggestions, which we'll discuss in detail later.

The core of successful keyword research is understanding search intent. What are people *actually* searching for when they use a particular keyword? Are they looking for information, to buy a product, to compare options, or something else entirely? Consider the keyword "best Italian restaurant." Someone searching for this phrase likely isn't just looking for a list of restaurants; they're looking for recommendations and reviews to help them decide where to dine. Understanding this intent allows you to craft content that directly addresses their needs.

This brings us to the importance of long-tail keywords. These are longer, more specific phrases that often have lower competition but higher conversion potential. Instead of focusing on broad keywords like "shoes" or "restaurants," long-tail keywords delve into specifics, such as "vegan leather shoes for women size 7" or "romantic Italian restaurant with outdoor seating in Chicago." These highly targeted keywords attract a more qualified audience, increasing the likelihood of conversions. Think about your own search habits; you're more likely to use long-tail keywords when conducting detailed research. Replicating this specificity in your keyword strategy is paramount.

Let's examine some practical examples. Suppose you run a small organic coffee shop. While keywords like "coffee" or "coffee shop" have high search volume, they are incredibly competitive. Instead, you might focus on long-tail keywords like "best organic coffee near me," "specialty coffee beans online," "organic fair trade coffee delivery," or "cold brew coffee recipe." These keywords are far more targeted and less competitive, allowing your website to rank higher in search results for a more relevant audience.

Similarly, a freelance graphic designer might target long-tail keywords like "affordable logo design for startups," "professional brochure design services," or "website design for small businesses in Austin, Texas." These specific keywords attract clients who are actively searching for their particular niche services, improving the quality of leads generated.

Beyond identifying suitable keywords, understanding keyword difficulty is crucial. Tools like Ahrefs and SEMrush provide metrics to assess how difficult it is to rank for a given keyword. This involves analyzing the websites currently ranking for that keyword, considering factors like their domain authority, backlink profile, and content quality. Targeting keywords with high search volume and low difficulty is the ideal scenario, although it is not always attainable. Focus on achievable targets while still striving for higher search volume. You might start with keywords with slightly higher difficulty but still within reach. The key is to start small, achieve success, and progressively target keywords of higher difficulty.

Once you've identified your target keywords, the next step is integrating them naturally into your website content. This is where many fall short. Avoid keyword stuffing, which involves cramming keywords into your content regardless of context or readability. Search engines penalize this practice, negatively impacting your rankings. Instead, focus on creating high-quality, informative content that naturally incorporates your keywords. Write as you would speak to a customer; focus on creating engaging, helpful content that adds value. The keywords should serve the content, not the other way around.

Consider a blog post about the health benefits of organic coffee. Instead of forcing keywords like "organic coffee beans" repeatedly, integrate them naturally within the text, such as "the rich aroma of freshly roasted organic coffee beans," or "the health benefits of choosing organic coffee beans over conventionally grown coffee." The keyword is present without disrupting the flow or readability of the text.

Effective keyword research isn't a one-time event; it's an ongoing process. Regularly monitor your keyword rankings and search volume. New keywords may emerge, while the performance of others may decline. Your keyword strategy should be dynamic and adaptive, constantly evolving to reflect changes in search trends and user behavior. Tools like Google Search Console provide valuable data on the keywords your website is already ranking for, giving you further insights into user search patterns.

Furthermore, analyzing your competitors' keyword strategies provides valuable insights. See what keywords your competitors are targeting and how they're performing. This information can help identify opportunities for your own website. This competitive analysis isn't about copying; it's about learning and identifying gaps in the market. Maybe you can target keywords your competitors are neglecting, or perhaps you can offer a different perspective on already popular keywords.

Ultimately, effective keyword research and targeting are about understanding your audience, their search behavior, and your competitive landscape. It's a combination of using the right tools, understanding search intent, and creating high-quality content that naturally incorporates relevant keywords. This approach, combined with consistent monitoring and optimization, forms the foundation for a successful SEO strategy that drives organic traffic and ultimately contributes to business growth. Remember, sustainable success in online marketing is built on a foundation of understanding and responding to the needs of your potential customers. Keyword research is the first, critical step in that process.

OnPage Optimization Techniques

On-page optimization is the art of fine-tuning individual web pages to make them more appealing to both search engines and users. It's the next crucial step after laying the groundwork with effective keyword research. Think of it as meticulously crafting each page of your online storefront to ensure maximum visibility and attractiveness to potential customers. This involves optimizing various elements, ensuring each contributes to a seamless and effective user experience while simultaneously signaling relevance to search engine algorithms.

One of the most critical elements is the title tag. This short snippet of text, usually appearing as the blue clickable link in search engine results pages (SERPs), acts as a headline for your page. It needs to be both concise and compelling, accurately reflecting the page's content while including your primary keyword. Avoid overly long title tags, as search engines truncate them, potentially losing valuable keyword placement and essential information. Aim for a length around 50-60 characters to ensure the entire title displays clearly on most SERPs. A well-crafted title tag entices users to click, increasing your click-through rate (CTR), a key ranking factor.

For example, a page about organic dog treats might have a title tag like "Best Organic Dog Treats for Sensitive Stomachs | [Your Brand Name]". This title clearly communicates the page's content, incorporates relevant keywords ("organic dog treats," "sensitive stomachs"), and includes the brand name for brand reinforcement. Compare that to a less effective title like "Dog Treats," which lacks specificity and fails to capture the unique selling proposition.

The meta description, though not a direct ranking factor, significantly impacts CTR. This brief summary, usually appearing under the title tag in SERPs, provides a concise overview of your page's content. While search engines might modify the displayed meta description, crafting a compelling and accurate one is crucial for enticing users to click. Use strong action words, highlight key benefits, and incorporate your primary keywords naturally, again aiming for brevity and clarity. A well-written meta description can increase organic traffic substantially by boosting your CTR.

Continuing with our dog treat example, a compelling meta description could read: "Discover the healthiest, most delicious organic dog treats for sensitive pups! Made with all-natural ingredients, our treats are perfect for picky eaters. Shop now and see the difference!" This description clearly communicates the benefits, uses persuasive language, and incorporates relevant keywords, making it far more attractive than a generic description.

Header tags (H1-H6) play a vital role in both SEO and user experience. The H1 tag serves as the main headline for your page and should contain your primary keyword. Subsequent header tags (H2-H6) should organize your content hierarchically, using relevant keywords where appropriate. Proper header tag usage improves readability and provides clear structural signals to search engines, indicating the page's topic and organization. Consistent and logical use of header tags enhances both SEO and UX.

In our example, the H1 tag could be "Organic Dog Treats for Sensitive Stomachs," while H2 tags might include "Why Choose Organic?", "Ingredients We Use," and "Customer Testimonials." Each header tag should reflect a logical section of the page, improving readability and usability, factors that search engines also consider.

Image optimization is another crucial aspect of on-page SEO. Search engines cannot directly "see" images; they rely on alt text to understand their content. Accurate and descriptive alt text not only makes your images accessible to visually impaired users but also provides valuable context for search engines. Use relevant keywords in your alt text, describing the image accurately and concisely. Optimizing image file sizes further improves page load speed, a critical ranking factor. Smaller images load faster, leading to better user experience and improved search engine rankings.

Internal linking connects pages within your website, creating a navigational structure that enhances user experience and boosts SEO. Linking relevant pages together improves site architecture, allowing search engines to crawl and index your content more effectively. This not only enhances navigation for users but also distributes link equity throughout your site, strengthening the overall SEO. Strategic internal linking increases engagement and time spent on your website, positively influencing search engine rankings.

Tools and plugins can simplify the process of on-page optimization. Plugins like Yoast SEO for WordPress provide comprehensive guidance and automation for optimizing title tags, meta descriptions, and header tags. These tools frequently analyze your content, suggesting improvements and flagging potential issues. They can automate much of the tedious task of on-page optimization, allowing you to focus on creating compelling content. However, these tools should be considered supportive aids, not replacements for careful manual review and optimization.

Successful on-page optimization is about striking a balance between user experience and search engine optimization. It's not about tricking search engines; it's about creating high-quality content that both users and search engines find valuable. By focusing on creating an intuitive and engaging website while carefully incorporating relevant keywords, you can significantly improve your search engine rankings and drive more organic traffic to your website, ultimately leading to business growth. Remember, consistent monitoring and adaptation are key to maintaining and improving your on-page SEO performance. Regularly review your website's performance, analyze your keyword rankings, and adjust your strategy based on your findings. The world of SEO is dynamic; constant adaptation is crucial for sustainable success.

OffPage Optimization Strategies

Off-page optimization is the crucial next step after mastering on-page techniques. While on-page SEO focuses on optimizing elements within your website, off-page optimization concentrates on building your website's authority and reputation across the broader internet. Think of it as building your website's credibility and influence outside its own walls. This involves a range of activities aimed at earning valuable backlinks from reputable sources, increasing brand awareness, and fostering engagement across different platforms. Successful off-page optimization significantly impacts your search engine rankings and drives organic traffic.

One of the most effective off-page optimization strategies is link building. Backlinks are essentially votes of confidence from other websites. When a reputable website links to yours, search engines interpret this as a positive endorsement, boosting your website's authority and ranking potential. However, the quality of backlinks matters more than quantity. A single high-quality backlink from a trusted, relevant website carries far more weight than hundreds of low-quality backlinks from spammy sources.

Building high-quality backlinks requires a strategic approach. You shouldn't aim for sheer volume; instead, focus on earning links from websites that align with your niche and target audience. This might involve reaching out to bloggers and influencers in your industry, creating high-quality content that naturally attracts links, or participating in relevant online communities. Guest blogging, for instance, is an excellent way to earn backlinks while simultaneously building brand awareness and establishing yourself as a thought leader in your field. By contributing valuable content to other websites, you not only gain exposure to a new audience but also secure a valuable backlink to your website.

Remember to always prioritize quality over quantity when pursuing guest blogging opportunities. Focus on websites with a high domain authority and a relevant audience. A guest post on a low-quality website with irrelevant content won't benefit your SEO and could even harm your rankings. Ensure the content you create is high-quality, engaging, and informative – something that will genuinely resonate with the target audience of the host website. Moreover, natural link building is key; avoid using unnatural or manipulative methods that could lead to penalties from search engines.

Beyond guest blogging, there are many other effective link-building strategies. Participating in relevant online forums and communities allows you to share your expertise and subtly introduce links to your website when appropriate. Contributing insightful comments and actively participating in discussions establish you as a knowledgeable member of the community, increasing your visibility and credibility. However, remember to participate authentically and avoid spammy or self-promotional behavior.

Broken link building is another less common but powerful technique. This involves identifying broken links on relevant websites and offering your own content as a replacement. By contacting the website owner and suggesting your resource as a suitable alternative, you can secure a valuable backlink while simultaneously assisting the website in maintaining its quality. This strategy demonstrates your helpfulness and expertise, further enhancing your website's reputation.

Directory submissions can also play a role in off-page optimization. Submitting your website to relevant online directories can increase your website's visibility and generate backlinks. While directory submissions may not be as impactful as other link-building strategies, they still offer a valuable way to increase your online presence and acquire backlinks from reputable sources. However, ensure that the directories you submit to are relevant to your niche and have a high domain authority; avoid low-quality directories, which may not provide any SEO benefit and could even negatively affect your rankings.

Social media marketing is another essential aspect of off-page optimization. While social media signals aren't a direct ranking factor in the same way as backlinks, they influence your website's visibility and can indirectly boost your SEO. A strong social media presence increases brand awareness, generates traffic to your website, and fosters engagement with your target audience. This engagement leads to more shares and mentions, which can lead to more backlinks and increased brand visibility. A vibrant and engaging social media presence creates a positive cycle, indirectly improving your SEO performance. Consistency and quality are crucial for social media success. Regularly posting valuable and engaging content keeps your audience involved and encourages sharing and interaction.

Furthermore, building relationships with influencers in your industry can significantly enhance your off-page optimization efforts. Influencers have established audiences and credibility, and their endorsements can significantly boost your brand's visibility and reach. Collaborating with influencers through sponsored posts, giveaways, or joint content creation allows you to tap into their established networks, gaining access to a wider audience and potentially earning valuable backlinks. However, ensure you choose influencers who align with your brand's values and target audience.

Beyond these strategies, several other tactics contribute to effective off-page optimization. Participating in online events, such as webinars or conferences, offers opportunities to network, build relationships, and increase brand awareness. This exposure creates opportunities for backlinks and strengthens your website's authority within your industry. Creating high-quality, shareable content, such as infographics or videos, is another effective way to increase brand visibility and earn backlinks. By producing content that is both informative and visually appealing, you attract a larger audience and encourage sharing, leading to increased organic traffic and potentially valuable backlinks.

Measuring the effectiveness of your off-page optimization efforts is crucial for optimizing your strategy and maximizing your ROI. Tools like SEMrush and Ahrefs provide comprehensive insights into your backlink profile, allowing you to track your progress, identify areas for improvement, and analyze the effectiveness of different strategies. By regularly monitoring your backlink profile, you gain a clear understanding of which strategies are working and which need adjustment. Analyzing the quality of your backlinks, their source websites, and the anchor text used helps determine the impact of your efforts on your search engine rankings.

Off-page optimization is an ongoing process that requires continuous effort and adaptation. There is no one-size-fits-all solution; the most effective strategy varies depending on your industry, target audience, and specific goals. Consistency is key. Regularly implement and refine your off-page optimization strategies to maintain and improve your website's authority and search engine rankings. The results may not be immediate, but consistent effort over time will yield significant returns in terms of organic traffic and increased brand visibility. Remember, the ultimate goal is to build a strong online reputation and establish your website as a trusted and authoritative source of information in your niche. By combining effective on-page and off-page optimization strategies, you create a synergistic effect, maximizing your website's potential and achieving significant organic growth.

Technical SEO Best Practices

Technical SEO, often overlooked, forms the bedrock of a successful online presence. While off-page optimization builds external authority, technical SEO ensures your website is easily accessible and understood by search engines. It's the foundation upon which all other SEO efforts are built. A technically sound website not only improves your search engine rankings but also enhances user experience, leading to higher engagement and conversion rates. Neglecting technical SEO is like building a house on shaky ground; it might stand for a while, but it's prone to collapse under pressure.

One of the most crucial aspects of technical SEO is website speed. Search engines prioritize websites that load quickly. Slow loading times frustrate users, leading to high bounce rates and lower engagement. Google's Core Web Vitals, a set of metrics measuring user experience, directly impacts your search rankings. These metrics include Largest Contentful Paint (LCP), Cumulative Layout Shift (CLS), and First Input Delay (FID). LCP measures how quickly the main content of your page loads, CLS quantifies visual instability during page load, and FID reflects the responsiveness of your page to user interactions. Optimizing these metrics is crucial for a positive user experience and improved search engine rankings.

Several factors contribute to slow loading times. Large image files, unoptimized code, and inefficient server configurations are common culprits. Optimizing images by compressing them without sacrificing quality is a straightforward way to improve loading speed. Utilizing tools like TinyPNG or ImageOptim can significantly reduce image file sizes without noticeable visual degradation. Minifying CSS and JavaScript files removes unnecessary characters from your code, reducing file sizes and improving load times. Content Delivery Networks (CDNs) distribute your website's content across multiple servers globally, ensuring faster loading times for users in different geographic locations. Investing in a high-performance hosting provider with optimized server infrastructure is also crucial.

Mobile-friendliness is another critical aspect of technical SEO. With the increasing use of mobile devices, ensuring your website is easily accessible and usable on all screen sizes is essential. Google's mobile-first indexing means Google primarily uses the mobile version of your website for indexing and ranking. A poorly designed mobile website leads to a negative user experience, impacting your search engine rankings and conversion rates. Responsive web design, which adapts your website's layout to different screen sizes, is the best approach to mobile optimization. Using a responsive theme or framework ensures your website provides a seamless experience across all devices.

Beyond responsive design, mobile optimization involves ensuring your website is easily navigable and that all elements are appropriately sized and positioned for mobile screens. Large text sizes, clear call-to-action buttons, and simplified navigation menus enhance user experience on mobile devices. Testing your website's mobile-friendliness using Google's Mobile-Friendly Test tool provides valuable insights into areas needing improvement. Addressing any identified issues ensures a positive mobile user experience, which directly impacts your search engine rankings.

XML sitemaps are crucial for helping search engines crawl and index your website effectively. A sitemap provides search engine bots with a complete list of all the pages on your website, making it easier for them to discover and index your content. Creating a sitemap is relatively straightforward and can be accomplished using online tools or through plugins for your content management system. Submitting your sitemap to Google Search Console ensures Google is aware of your website's structure and content.

Robots.txt, another essential element of technical SEO, allows you to control which parts of your website are accessible to search engine crawlers. This is particularly useful for excluding pages under construction, sensitive content, or duplicate content. Creating a well-structured robots.txt file helps prevent search engine bots from wasting time crawling unnecessary pages, allowing them to focus on your important content. Incorrectly configured robots.txt files can inadvertently block access to important pages, hindering your SEO efforts. Regularly reviewing and updating your robots.txt file is crucial to ensure it's accurately reflecting your website's structure and content.

Schema markup is a form of structured data that helps search engines understand the content on your website. Using schema markup enhances the visibility of your website in search results, providing rich snippets that include ratings, reviews, prices, and other relevant information. This improved visibility attracts more clicks and increases traffic to your website. Implementing schema markup is typically done through adding specific code to your website's HTML. Numerous online tools and resources help generate the necessary code for different types of content.

Structured data improves search result presentation, allowing for rich snippets which contain additional data about your website displayed in the search engine results page, making your site stand out from the competition. By adding schema markup, search engines understand the context and nature of your content, potentially resulting in higher rankings and increased click-through rates. Implementing schema is a worthwhile technical SEO task that benefits both search engine and user experience.

Website security is paramount. Search engines prioritize secure websites (HTTPS) over insecure ones (HTTP). An HTTPS certificate ensures data transmitted between your website and users is encrypted, protecting sensitive information like credit card details or personal data. Implementing HTTPS enhances trust and security, both crucial for a positive user experience and improved search engine rankings. Google's Search Console provides tools to check for security issues and confirms your HTTPS setup.

Internal linking is also a significant technical SEO aspect. Internally linking relevant pages on your website helps search engine bots navigate your website and discover new content. It also improves user experience by providing easy access to related information. However, creating too many links can negatively impact your website's speed, making careful selection and placement vital. An effective internal linking strategy ensures your website's structure is clear to both search engines and users. Use descriptive anchor text and contextually relevant links to enhance the user experience.

Regularly analyzing your website's performance using website analytics tools is crucial for identifying and addressing technical SEO issues. Google Analytics provides comprehensive insights into website traffic, user behavior, and conversion rates. Monitoring key metrics like page loading speed, bounce rate, and mobile traffic allows you to identify areas needing improvement. Addressing these issues proactively ensures your website maintains good technical

SEO health, which translates to improved search engine rankings and organic traffic. Monitoring and interpreting data is critical to adapting and refining the technical strategy.

By addressing these technical SEO best practices, you enhance your website's visibility, user experience, and overall SEO effectiveness. It's a continuous process of optimization and improvement; ongoing monitoring and adaptation are key to maintaining a high-performing, technically sound website. Remember, technical SEO isn't a one-time task; it's an ongoing commitment that forms the cornerstone of a successful online strategy.

Measuring and Analyzing SEO Results

Measuring and analyzing the results of your SEO efforts is not a one-time event; it's an ongoing process crucial for understanding what's working and what's not. This continuous monitoring allows you to refine your strategy, maximize your return on investment (ROI), and ultimately achieve sustainable growth. Without this crucial step, your SEO efforts become a shot in the dark, with no way to gauge effectiveness or identify areas needing improvement.

The cornerstone of effective SEO measurement lies in leveraging robust analytics tools. Google Analytics is the industry standard, offering a comprehensive suite of tools to track website traffic, user behavior, and conversion rates. It provides granular data on various aspects of your online presence, allowing you to identify patterns, trends, and areas for optimization. Understanding how to interpret this data is as important as gathering it.

Google Analytics offers a plethora of metrics to track. Let's explore some key metrics and how to interpret them effectively:

Website Traffic: Monitor the overall volume of traffic to your website, paying close attention to its source. Is your traffic predominantly organic (from search engines), or are you heavily reliant on paid advertising or social media referrals? A healthy balance is ideal, demonstrating a robust and diversified approach. Significant drops in organic traffic might signal an issue requiring attention, such as a Google algorithm update or a technical issue on your website. Conversely, a sustained increase in organic traffic signifies that your SEO efforts are bearing fruit.

Keyword Rankings: Track your website's ranking for your target keywords. Use tools like SEMrush, Ahrefs, or Moz to monitor your position on Google's search engine results pages (SERPs). A steady rise in ranking for your primary keywords signifies that your optimization efforts are succeeding. If rankings are stagnating or declining, it signals a need for reevaluation and potential adjustment to your strategy. Focus on long-tail keywords (more specific, longer phrases) which can often have less competition, resulting in easier ranking opportunities.

Bounce Rate: This metric indicates the percentage of visitors who leave your website after viewing only one page. A high bounce rate suggests potential issues with your website's content, design, or overall user experience. A low bounce rate suggests that users find your content engaging and valuable, leading them to explore your site further. Analyzing landing pages with high bounce rates can reveal content quality problems, poor user interface design, or irrelevant keywords.

Conversion Rate: This metric measures the percentage of visitors who complete a desired action, such as making a purchase, signing up for a newsletter, or filling out a contact form. This metric directly correlates with your business goals. A low conversion rate might signal that your website isn't effectively guiding users toward desired actions. A/B testing of call-to-action buttons, improving site navigation, and optimizing the checkout process can improve conversion rates.

Time on Site: This metric indicates the average time visitors spend on your website. A longer average time on site suggests engaging and valuable content that keeps users interested. Conversely, a short average time on site may indicate unengaging content or poor website design. Analyzing individual pages allows for identifying potential areas where user engagement can be improved.

Beyond Google Analytics, several other tools provide valuable insights into your SEO performance. Google Search Console offers detailed information about how Google crawls and indexes your website. It provides data on crawl errors, index coverage issues, and the keywords your website ranks for. Using this data in conjunction with Google Analytics allows for a holistic understanding of your SEO performance.

Other SEO tools, such as SEMrush, Ahrefs, and Moz, offer advanced features for keyword research, competitor analysis, and backlink analysis. These platforms provide deeper insights into your website's SEO performance and help identify opportunities for improvement. These tools often come with a price tag; however, many offer free trials or limited free versions, which can be valuable for smaller businesses.

Interpreting data from these tools requires analytical thinking and a willingness to adjust your strategies based on the evidence. Avoid making knee-jerk reactions to short-term fluctuations in data. Instead, look for patterns and trends over time. For instance, a sudden drop in rankings for a particular keyword might be due to a temporary algorithm update, rather than a flaw in your strategy. Sustained decline, however, indicates a need to re-evaluate the keyword, content, or website architecture.

Setting realistic expectations is crucial. SEO is a long-term game, not a quick fix. Don't expect overnight success. It takes time and consistent effort to build a strong online presence. Patience is vital; consistent effort over time is more effective than sporadic bursts of activity.

Regularly review and adjust your SEO strategy based on the data you gather. This iterative process ensures your efforts remain focused and effective. For instance, if you find that a particular keyword is not performing well, you might need to re-optimize the content associated with that keyword, or replace it with a more relevant term. Continuously analyze your competition and adapt your strategies accordingly. Success requires staying up-to-date on industry trends and best practices.

In conclusion, measuring and analyzing SEO results is an integral part of a successful online strategy. Leveraging analytics tools, interpreting data, and adapting your strategy based on the evidence provides valuable insight into your SEO effectiveness, ensuring you are investing your time and resources wisely. This data-driven approach helps you refine your efforts, optimize your website, and ultimately achieve sustainable online growth. Remember, SEO is an ongoing process, requiring continuous monitoring, adjustment, and a commitment to consistent improvement.

Choosing the Right Social Media Platforms

Choosing the right social media platforms is paramount to a successful online marketing strategy. It's not about being everywhere; it's about being *where your audience is* and where your message resonates most effectively. Throwing resources at every platform indiscriminately is a recipe for wasted time and money. A focused, targeted approach yields far better results.

Let's examine some of the most popular platforms and their unique characteristics. Understanding these nuances allows you to select the channels that best align with your business goals and your target audience's online behavior.

Facebook: Facebook remains a marketing powerhouse, boasting a vast user base across demographics. Its robust advertising platform allows for highly targeted campaigns, enabling you to reach specific audiences based on factors such as age, location, interests, and behavior. Facebook also offers features like Facebook Groups, which can foster community engagement and brand loyalty. However, organic reach on Facebook has decreased significantly, meaning that relying solely on organic content to reach a substantial audience can be challenging. Successful Facebook strategies often incorporate a blend of organic posting and paid advertising. For example, a local bakery could utilize Facebook to promote daily specials, run contests to engage followers, and leverage targeted advertising to reach people within a specific radius interested in baking or desserts. They might also use Facebook Groups to create a community where customers can share recipes and connect with the bakery.

Instagram: Instagram is a highly visual platform ideal for showcasing products or services through compelling images and videos. Its emphasis on aesthetics makes it particularly well-suited for businesses in industries like fashion, food, travel, and beauty. Influencer marketing is a powerful tool on Instagram, allowing businesses to partner with relevant influencers to reach wider audiences. Instagram's shopping features facilitate direct sales, enabling users to purchase products directly through the app. A clothing boutique, for instance, could leverage Instagram's visual appeal to showcase new arrivals, style different outfits, and engage with followers through polls and stories. Influencer collaborations could further extend their reach to a wider fashion-conscious audience. Effective use of hashtags is crucial for discoverability on Instagram.

Twitter: Twitter is a platform for real-time updates, news, and discussions. Its short-form nature makes it ideal for quick announcements, engaging in conversations, and responding promptly to customer inquiries. Twitter's trending topics can provide valuable insight into current conversations and help businesses identify opportunities to participate in relevant discussions. A tech startup, for example, might use Twitter to announce product launches, share industry news, engage in discussions about relevant topics, and quickly address customer service issues. The rapid-fire nature of Twitter requires quick thinking and a consistent presence to maintain engagement.

LinkedIn: LinkedIn is primarily a professional networking platform, making it invaluable for businesses in B2B (business-to-business) sectors. It allows for professional profile creation, connecting with potential clients and partners, sharing industry insights, and participating in relevant discussions. LinkedIn's advertising platform allows for highly targeted campaigns reaching specific professional demographics. A consulting firm, for instance, could use LinkedIn to showcase its expertise, network with potential clients, and share insightful content related to their industry. They could also use LinkedIn's advertising features to target specific job titles or industries.

TikTok: TikTok's short-form video format has gained immense popularity, particularly among younger audiences. Its algorithm favors engaging content, making it a platform where viral potential is relatively high. However, success on TikTok requires creativity, understanding the platform's unique trends and culture, and developing highly engaging video content. A dance studio, for example, could use TikTok to showcase dance routines, participate in trending challenges, and build a community around dance enthusiasts. Their success would depend on creating visually compelling and engaging videos that resonate with TikTok's audience.

Pinterest: Pinterest is a visual discovery platform, enabling users to save and organize images and ideas. It's particularly effective for businesses with visually appealing products or services. Pinterest allows for the creation of rich pins, which provide more detailed information about products, making it ideal for e-commerce businesses. A home décor company, for instance, could use Pinterest to showcase their products in styled settings, providing ideas and inspiration for home improvement projects. Effective use of keywords and descriptions is crucial for discoverability on Pinterest.

YouTube: YouTube is a massive video-sharing platform, providing opportunities for businesses to create engaging video content, such as product demos, tutorials, and behind-the-scenes glimpses. YouTube's algorithm prioritizes video watch time, meaning creating compelling and engaging videos is crucial. A cooking channel, for example, could use YouTube to create recipe videos, food reviews, and cooking tutorials, building an audience of food enthusiasts. They could also monetize their channel through advertising or sponsorships.

Choosing the right platforms depends on several factors:

Target Audience: Where does your ideal customer spend their time online? Research your target audience's online behavior to identify the platforms they frequent.

Business Goals: What are you trying to achieve with your social media marketing? Are you aiming to increase brand awareness, drive sales, generate leads, or build community? Different platforms are better suited to different goals.

Resources: How much time and budget do you have to dedicate to social media marketing? Managing multiple platforms requires significant resources. Starting with one or two platforms and expanding gradually is often a more effective strategy.

Content Strategy: What kind of content are you best suited to create and share? Are you comfortable producing high-quality videos, or are you more comfortable writing blog posts? Different platforms require different content formats.

Once you've identified the platforms best suited to your business, develop a consistent content strategy, engage with your followers, and track your results. Regularly analyze your performance to ensure you are optimizing your efforts. Remember, social media marketing is an ongoing process; adapt and adjust your approach based on the data you gather. The key is consistent engagement, meaningful interactions, and a deep understanding of your target audience. The platforms are merely the tools; the strategy and execution are what truly drive success. Don't chase fleeting trends; focus on building a sustainable and authentic online presence that resonates with your audience and aligns with your business goals.

Creating Engaging Social Media Content

Creating engaging social media content is the cornerstone of a successful social media marketing strategy. It's not enough to simply post; you need to create content that captures attention, sparks interest, and encourages interaction. This requires a deep understanding of your target audience, the platforms you're using, and the types of content that resonate most effectively. Let's delve into the key elements of crafting compelling social media content.

First and foremost, understand your audience. Who are you trying to reach? What are their interests, values, and pain points? Tailoring your content to resonate with your specific target audience is crucial. Generic content rarely achieves significant engagement. For example, if you're targeting young professionals interested in sustainable living, your content should reflect that—perhaps showcasing eco-friendly products, highlighting sustainable practices, or sharing inspiring stories about environmental activism. In contrast, if your target audience is senior citizens interested in travel, your content should focus on accessible travel options, showcasing destinations with minimal physical exertion, or sharing tips for comfortable and safe travel.

Once you understand your audience, consider the various content formats available. Text-based updates are suitable for quick announcements, sharing links to blog posts, or engaging in conversations. However, in today's visually-driven world, images and videos are often more impactful. High-quality images can capture attention quickly, conveying your message in a visually compelling way. A beautifully photographed product, an eye-catching graphic, or a captivating landscape image can all effectively communicate your brand message and engage your audience. For example, a restaurant might share appetizing photos of their dishes, while a clothing retailer could post stylish pictures of models wearing their clothes.

Videos, meanwhile, are particularly powerful for storytelling and demonstrating products or services. They can be short, engaging clips showcasing behind-the-scenes glimpses of your business, or longer, more in-depth tutorials or product demonstrations. For instance, a makeup company could create short video tutorials demonstrating how to apply their products, while a software company could produce a longer video explaining the features and benefits of their software. Short-form videos, especially those under 60 seconds, are incredibly effective for quick engagement, and platforms like TikTok and Instagram Reels are ideal for this format.

The use of stories—fleeting, temporary posts—provides a less formal and more intimate way to connect with your audience. Stories allow for greater spontaneity and immediacy, enabling you to share updates, behind-the-scenes looks, quick polls, and informal interactions with your followers. For example, a bookstore might use stories to announce upcoming author events, showcase new book arrivals, or share glimpses of their daily operations. A fitness instructor could use stories to share quick workout tips, announce upcoming classes, or engage followers with polls about preferred workout types.

Regardless of the content format, optimizing your content for the specific platform is essential. Each platform has its own nuances and user expectations. What works well on Instagram might not work as effectively on LinkedIn. For example, visual content tends to perform exceptionally well on Instagram and Pinterest, while text-based content is frequently more effective on Twitter and LinkedIn.

Understanding these platform-specific nuances is key to optimizing your content strategy for maximum impact.

Hashtags are a vital tool for increasing the discoverability of your content. They categorize your posts, making them easier for users to find when searching for specific topics or interests. However, it's essential to use relevant and targeted hashtags. Overusing hashtags or using irrelevant ones can be detrimental to your reach and engagement. Research relevant hashtags in your industry and use a mix of broad and niche hashtags to maximize your reach.

Visually appealing content is also vital. Ensure that your images and videos are high-quality, well-lit, and visually engaging. Consistency in your branding—using consistent colors, fonts, and imagery—is essential to create a cohesive and recognizable brand identity. This consistency strengthens brand recognition and helps you stand out amidst the clutter of social media feeds.

In addition to creating engaging content, it's vital to interact with your audience. Respond to comments, answer questions, and participate in relevant conversations. This builds community, fosters engagement, and demonstrates that you're actively listening to your audience. Regularly monitor your social media channels for comments, mentions, and direct messages, ensuring that your responses are timely and informative.

Finally, analyze your results. Track your engagement metrics —likes, comments, shares, and website clicks—to gauge the effectiveness of your content. Use this data to inform your future content strategy, adjusting your approach based on what works best and what needs improvement. What kind of content receives the most engagement? What types of posts generate the most website traffic or lead conversions? This data-driven approach is vital for continually optimizing your social media marketing strategy for maximum impact.

For instance, a small business owner selling handcrafted jewelry might experiment with different types of content on Instagram. They could post high-quality product photos, short videos showcasing their crafting process, behind-the-scenes glimpses of their workspace, and user-generated content featuring customers wearing their jewelry. By tracking the engagement metrics for each type of post, they can determine which content resonates most effectively with their target audience and allocate resources accordingly. Perhaps they discover that videos showing the crafting process generate significantly higher engagement than static product photos. This insight informs their future content strategy, leading them to prioritize video creation.

Another example might involve a local coffee shop. They could leverage Facebook to run contests, engage with their community through polls and questions, and showcase their new coffee blends with visually appealing photos. On Instagram, they could share aesthetically pleasing pictures of their coffee creations and the ambiance of their shop, using relevant hashtags to reach a wider audience. They might also use stories to offer daily specials, provide behind-the-scenes glimpses of their operations, and interact directly with customers. By consistently creating engaging content and analyzing their results, they can refine their social media strategy to build a loyal customer base and expand their business.

Remember, creating engaging social media content is an ongoing process of experimentation, refinement, and adaptation. Don't be afraid to try new things, analyze your results, and adjust your approach accordingly. Consistency, authenticity, and a deep understanding of your target audience are the keys to success in social media marketing. Focus on building relationships, adding value, and creating content that truly resonates with your audience – this is far more sustainable than chasing fleeting viral trends.

Building a Loyal Social Media Following

Building a loyal social media following isn't about chasing viral fame; it's about cultivating genuine connections with your audience. It requires a consistent, strategic approach that goes beyond simply posting content. This involves actively engaging with your followers, fostering a sense of community, and providing value that resonates with their interests and needs. Let's explore several proven strategies to achieve this.

One highly effective method is running contests and giveaways. These create excitement and encourage interaction. A simple contest could involve asking users to like your post, tag three friends, and share it to their story for a chance to win a prize relevant to your brand or industry. For instance, a clothing brand might offer a gift card to their store, while a technology company could give away the latest gadget. Contests drive engagement by incentivizing users to interact with your content and spread the word about your brand. Remember to clearly outline the rules, the prize, and the timeline for the contest to ensure transparency and avoid any confusion. Platforms like Instagram and Facebook are particularly well-suited for this type of engagement-driven strategy.

Beyond contests, actively interacting with your followers is crucial. Responding promptly and thoughtfully to comments and messages demonstrates that you value your audience's input. This simple act of engagement significantly strengthens the relationship you have with your followers, transforming casual viewers into loyal supporters. When someone takes the time to comment on your post, acknowledging their comment and engaging in a conversation shows that you're actively listening. Consider asking questions in your posts to encourage further discussion, responding to their comments, and using their feedback to inform your future content strategy. This creates a sense of dialogue and mutual understanding, fostering a positive and engaging social media environment. Remember that consistent interaction is key; sporadic responses can have a negative impact.

Another key aspect of cultivating a loyal following is leveraging the power of user-generated content. Encourage your customers or followers to share their experiences with your brand. This could involve reposting photos or videos they've shared using your products or services, featuring their testimonials in your stories, or creating a dedicated hashtag for users to share their content. User-generated content provides authentic and relatable content, increasing brand trust and engagement. It acts as a powerful social proof, showcasing how real people are positively interacting with your brand. For example, a restaurant might repost photos of customers enjoying their meals, while a clothing company could feature users modeling their clothes. Always remember to obtain permission before reposting user-generated content and to provide credit to the original creator.

Social media advertising can be a powerful tool for expanding your reach and targeting specific demographics. While organic reach is essential, strategically placed ads can significantly boost your visibility and connect with potential followers who haven't yet discovered your brand. Platforms like Facebook, Instagram, and Twitter offer sophisticated targeting options allowing you to reach specific audiences based on their interests, demographics, and online behavior. You can create visually appealing and engaging ad content designed to resonate with your target audience. Tracking your ad performance is key; analyzing metrics like impressions, clicks, and conversions helps refine your campaigns for optimal results. Remember to A/B test different ad creatives to see what resonates best with your audience.

Building a loyal following also necessitates embracing authenticity. Don't try to be someone you're not. Authenticity resonates with audiences, building trust and fostering genuine connections. Show the human side of your brand—share behind-the-scenes glimpses of your company culture, introduce your team, and showcase your values. This transparency builds a stronger connection with your audience, making them feel like they're part of a community. For example, a small business owner might share a post about the challenges and successes they've faced, fostering a sense of relatability and community. Authenticity is a long-term investment; it builds lasting relationships that are far more resilient than fleeting viral trends.

Consistency is paramount in building a successful social media presence. Regular posting keeps your audience engaged and maintains your brand's visibility. Develop a content calendar to ensure consistent posting across all platforms. This calendar should not just outline the content but also specify the timing of your posts, considering when your audience is most active. Consistency also applies to the style and tone of your content; maintain a consistent brand voice and aesthetic across all platforms to strengthen brand recognition and reinforce your brand's identity. This consistent presence keeps your brand top-of-mind for your followers, increasing the likelihood of engagement and loyalty.

In addition to consistent posting, analyzing your performance is vital. Track key metrics such as engagement rates, follower growth, website traffic from social media, and conversions. Regularly review these metrics to identify what's working well and what areas need improvement. Use this data to inform your future content strategy, refining your approach based on evidence and insights. For example, if you notice that videos perform better than static images, adjust your content calendar accordingly, dedicating more resources to video creation. This data-driven approach ensures your social media marketing efforts are constantly evolving and optimized for maximum impact.

Understanding the nuances of each platform is equally crucial. What works well on Instagram might not be as effective on LinkedIn. Tailor your content to the specific platform and its user base. Consider the visual style, the length of posts, and the types of content most popular on each platform. For example, short, engaging videos perform exceptionally well on TikTok and Instagram Reels, while thought leadership pieces are better suited for LinkedIn. This platform-specific approach enhances the effectiveness of your social media strategy, ensuring your message is delivered in the most effective manner.

Finally, remember that building a loyal social media following is a marathon, not a sprint. It requires patience, perseverance, and a genuine commitment to engaging with your audience. Don't get discouraged if you don't see results overnight. Consistent effort, genuine interaction, and a data-driven approach are the keys to building a strong and engaged community online. By focusing on fostering relationships, providing value, and consistently delivering engaging content, you can cultivate a loyal following that will support your brand's long-term growth and success. The key takeaway is that a sustainable online presence prioritizes quality engagement over fleeting viral moments. The strength of your online community is a testament to your long-term strategy, not a measure of instantaneous popularity.

Social Media Advertising and Paid Promotion

Social media advertising represents a powerful extension of your organic strategy, offering the ability to significantly amplify your reach and target specific demographics with precision. While organically building a loyal following is crucial for long-term success, paid promotion acts as a catalyst, accelerating the growth of your audience and driving engagement. This section delves into the practical aspects of creating and managing effective social media advertising campaigns, ensuring you maximize your return on investment (ROI).

The cornerstone of successful social media advertising lies in meticulous audience targeting. Each platform provides sophisticated tools to define your ideal customer, enabling you to deliver your message precisely to those most likely to be interested. Utilize demographic targeting, based on age, gender, location, and interests, to reach specific segments of your audience. Beyond demographics, consider interest-based targeting, focusing on individuals who have shown an affinity for subjects related to your brand or industry. This refined approach ensures your advertising budget is efficiently allocated, minimizing wasted impressions and maximizing engagement. For instance, a company selling organic skincare products would target users interested in healthy living, natural beauty, and sustainable products, rather than casting a wide net with generic demographic criteria.

Behavioral targeting provides another layer of sophistication. This approach allows you to reach individuals based on their online actions, such as website visits, app usage, or previous purchases. For instance, if someone has visited your website but hasn't made a purchase, you can retarget them with an ad featuring a special offer or discount, encouraging them to complete the transaction. This strategy leverages existing engagement, converting passive viewers into active customers. This retargeting approach has a higher conversion rate than broader campaigns because it targets individuals already familiar with your brand.

Once you've defined your target audience, crafting compelling ad creatives is paramount. The visual appeal and messaging of your ads must resonate with the audience's preferences and values. Use high-quality images or videos that showcase your product or service in the most appealing way. Consider A/B testing various creatives to determine which versions perform best—experiment with different visuals, headlines, and calls to action to optimize engagement and conversion rates. A compelling call to action, clearly stating the desired outcome (e.g., "Shop Now," "Learn More," "Sign Up"), is critical in driving user response. Ensure the visuals are consistent with your brand's overall aesthetic, reinforcing brand recognition and building brand awareness.

Selecting the right ad format is also vital, as each platform offers diverse options, each with its own strengths and weaknesses. Consider image ads for simple, impactful visuals, video ads for showcasing products in action, carousel ads to present multiple products or aspects of a single product, and story ads for engaging users in a more immersive format. The choice of ad format should be tailored to the specific platform and your campaign objectives. For example, short, engaging video ads are particularly effective on platforms like TikTok and Instagram Reels, whereas longer-form video ads may be more suitable for YouTube or Facebook.

Choosing the appropriate bidding strategy directly impacts your campaign's cost-effectiveness. Several bidding options are available, each influencing how much you pay per ad impression or click. Cost-per-click (CPC) bidding sets a maximum amount you're willing to pay each time someone clicks on your ad. Cost-per-mile (CPM) bidding sets a maximum price you're willing to pay for one thousand ad impressions, regardless of clicks. Consider your campaign goals when selecting a bidding strategy—CPC is often preferred for direct response campaigns aiming for conversions, whereas CPM might be more suitable for brand awareness campaigns aiming for broader reach. Experiment with different bidding strategies and closely monitor results to determine the most efficient approach.

Budget allocation is crucial for optimizing your return on investment. Start with a modest budget and gradually increase it as you learn what works best. Avoid pouring substantial resources into a campaign without proper testing and analysis. Allocate your budget strategically across different ad sets, allowing you to compare the performance of different targeting options and creatives. Regularly monitor your budget expenditure and adjust it as needed to maximize your reach and conversion rates. Consider setting daily or lifetime budgets, allowing you to control spending and prevent unexpected costs.

Measuring the results of your social media advertising campaigns is as critical as the campaign setup itself. Each platform provides detailed analytics dashboards that track key metrics such as impressions, clicks, reach, engagement, and conversions. Monitor these metrics closely to understand which campaigns are performing well and which require adjustments. Track your conversion rate, which indicates the percentage of users who click on your ad and complete a desired action (e.g., making a purchase, signing up for a newsletter). Pay close attention to your return on ad spend (ROAS), which measures the revenue generated for every dollar spent on advertising. Use this data to refine your targeting, adjust your bidding strategies, and optimize your ad creatives for better results. For instance, if you observe low conversion rates for a specific ad set, you may need to revise your targeting parameters or improve the call to action in your ad creative.

A/B testing is an integral part of optimizing your campaigns. Continuously test different elements of your ads, such as headlines, visuals, and calls to action, to identify which variations resonate best with your target audience. By systematically experimenting and analyzing the results, you can continuously improve the performance of your campaigns. For example, test different headlines to see which one has the highest click-through rate, or compare different images to see which one generates the most engagement. This iterative process of testing and refinement is essential for achieving optimal results from your social media advertising efforts.

Finally, integrating your social media advertising campaigns with other marketing channels amplifies their impact. For example, use retargeting ads to reach users who have interacted with your website or email campaigns. Consistent messaging and branding across all channels create a cohesive and impactful marketing strategy. Utilize the data gathered from your social media advertising campaigns to inform your overall marketing strategy. Analyzing audience behavior and engagement across various platforms provides valuable insights into optimizing your approach and maximizing your ROI.

By combining strategic audience targeting, compelling ad creatives, effective bidding strategies, budget management, performance measurement, and A/B testing, you can harness the power of social media advertising to significantly enhance your online presence, amplify your reach, and drive measurable business results. Remember that social media advertising is an ongoing process; continuous optimization and adaptation based on performance data are critical for sustained success. The key is to constantly refine your approach, learning from each campaign and iteratively improving your strategies to achieve your desired goals. This data-driven approach ensures that your social media advertising efforts remain efficient, cost-effective, and ultimately, highly successful in achieving your marketing objectives.

Analyzing Social Media Performance and ROI

Analyzing social media performance goes beyond simply observing an increase in followers or likes. It requires a deep dive into the data to understand what's truly working and what needs improvement. This involves using various metrics to assess the effectiveness of your strategies, identify areas for optimization, and ultimately, measure your return on investment (ROI). Without this crucial step, your social media efforts remain largely guesswork, hindering your ability to achieve your business objectives.

The first step in analyzing social media performance is choosing the right metrics. While vanity metrics like likes, shares, and follower count offer a superficial view, they don't necessarily translate to tangible business results. Instead, focus on metrics that directly relate to your goals. If your goal is to drive website traffic, track metrics like click-through rates (CTR) from your social media posts to your website. If your goal is to generate leads, monitor the number of form submissions or email sign-ups stemming from your social media activities. If your goal is to increase brand awareness, analyze metrics like reach and impressions, which indicate the total number of unique users who have seen your content.

Engagement metrics provide another crucial layer of insight. These metrics go beyond simple likes and shares, delving into the quality of interaction. Metrics like comments, shares, and saves indicate the level of audience interest and the virality of your content. A high engagement rate suggests your content resonates with your target audience and is likely to drive further organic reach. Conversely, low engagement may signal a need for content adjustments to better align with audience preferences. For instance, analyze the comments section to understand audience feedback, sentiment, and areas for improvement.

Reach and impressions offer a broader perspective on your content's visibility. Reach represents the number of unique users who have seen your content, while impressions reflect the total number of times your content has been displayed. Comparing these metrics provides insight into how effectively your content is reaching your target audience. A high reach with low engagement suggests your content might be attracting a broad audience but failing to capture their interest. Conversely, a low reach with high engagement points to a niche but highly engaged audience.

Conversion rates are crucial for measuring the effectiveness of your social media efforts in driving specific actions. This involves tracking the percentage of users who complete a desired action after engaging with your social media content, such as making a purchase, signing up for a newsletter, or requesting a quote. A high conversion rate indicates that your social media strategies are effectively guiding users towards desired outcomes. Tools like UTM parameters (Urchin Tracking Module) allow you to track the source of website traffic, enabling precise attribution to your social media campaigns.

Beyond individual post performance, consider analyzing overall campaign effectiveness. This requires a holistic view of your social media efforts, encompassing multiple posts, different platforms, and various content formats. Track key performance indicators (KPIs) across your entire social media strategy to identify trends, patterns, and areas for improvement. For example, analyze which platforms are driving the most engagement or conversions, which content formats resonate best with your audience, and which posting times yield the highest results.

Various analytical tools are available to assist in measuring social media performance. Each platform offers its own built-in analytics dashboard, providing valuable insights into user engagement and campaign performance. For example, Facebook Insights, Instagram Insights, and Twitter Analytics provide detailed data on various metrics, enabling you to track progress and make data-driven decisions. Beyond platform-specific analytics, consider third-party social media management tools that provide more comprehensive reporting and analytics features. These tools often offer features such as cross-platform reporting, campaign scheduling, and audience segmentation, greatly simplifying the process of monitoring and optimizing your social media presence.

To effectively utilize social media analytics, establish clear goals and key performance indicators (KPIs) at the outset. Without predefined goals, your analysis becomes a mere collection of data without a clear purpose or direction. Clearly defined KPIs ensure your efforts focus on relevant metrics that directly contribute to achieving your business objectives. These objectives might range from brand building and lead generation to direct sales and customer support. KPIs must directly relate to these objectives, allowing you to track progress and measure success.

Once you've gathered and analyzed your data, it's crucial to translate those findings into actionable insights. This involves identifying trends, patterns, and correlations within your data to determine what's working, what's not, and why. Data-driven decision making involves using this understanding to make informed adjustments to your social media strategies, refining your approach to optimize future campaigns and achieve better results. For example, if your data shows that video content consistently outperforms static images, adjust your content strategy to produce more video content. If particular posting times yield higher engagement, optimize your publishing schedule accordingly.

Reporting your social media performance is vital, both internally within your organization and externally to stakeholders. Create concise and visually appealing reports that present key findings and highlight successes and areas for improvement. These reports should focus on the most impactful metrics, clearly communicating the progress made and providing a roadmap for future actions. For internal reporting, reports may be more detailed, while external reports, for instance, to investors or clients, may require a more concise and summary-focused presentation.

Case studies of successful social media analytics and reporting offer valuable learning opportunities. Consider studying businesses within your industry that excel at using social media data to guide their strategies. Observe how they set objectives, choose their KPIs, analyze data, and translate these findings into actionable insights. Analyzing successful campaigns and identifying what made them work provides valuable inspiration and guidance for your own efforts. Examine their content strategies, engagement techniques, and use of social media analytics to understand their approach to success.

Analyzing social media performance isn't a one-time task; it's an ongoing process requiring continuous monitoring and adaptation. Regularly review your social media metrics, and conduct periodic in-depth analyses to track progress, identify emerging trends, and make informed adjustments to your strategies. Staying up-to-date on the latest social media algorithm updates and best practices ensures your campaigns remain efficient and effective. By making social media analytics an integral part of your overall marketing strategy, you transform data into actionable insights, optimizing your efforts and maximizing the return on your social media investment.

Building a Targeted Email List

Building a targeted email list is fundamental to successful email marketing. It's not just about accumulating numbers; it's about cultivating a community of engaged subscribers who genuinely want to hear from you. These individuals are more likely to convert into customers, brand advocates, and ultimately, contribute to the long-term growth of your business. This section will delve into the strategies for strategically building such a list, focusing on quality over quantity.

The cornerstone of any successful email list-building strategy is the lead magnet. A lead magnet is a valuable piece of content or offer that you provide in exchange for a subscriber's email address. Think of it as a compelling incentive, a reason for your audience to willingly give you their contact information. The effectiveness of your lead magnet directly impacts the quality and engagement of your email list. A poorly conceived lead magnet will attract subscribers who are not genuinely interested in your products or services, leading to low open rates, high unsubscribe rates, and ultimately, a wasted marketing effort.

Effective lead magnets should be highly relevant to your target audience and directly address their needs or pain points. Consider what problems your ideal customer faces and create a lead magnet that provides a solution or valuable information related to that problem. This could take many forms. For a business selling organic skincare products, a lead magnet could be an ebook titled "The Ultimate Guide to Achieving Radiant Skin Naturally." For a software company offering project management tools, a valuable lead magnet could be a checklist detailing the steps for effective project planning. For a fitness instructor, a free introductory workout video or a nutrition guide might be highly effective.

The format of your lead magnet is equally important. While ebooks and checklists remain popular choices, other formats can be equally effective depending on your target audience and the nature of your business. Consider these options:

Ebooks and White Papers: In-depth guides on specific topics related to your industry. These require significant effort but can offer high perceived value.
Checklists and Worksheets: Practical, actionable guides that help subscribers solve a specific problem. These are often quick to consume and highly effective.
Templates: Pre-designed documents that save subscribers time and effort. These could range from social media templates to email templates or budgeting spreadsheets.
Webinars and Online Courses: Interactive sessions that provide valuable information and establish a personal connection with your audience.
Discounts and Exclusive Offers: Straightforward incentives that can be highly effective, particularly for businesses selling products or services.
Free trials or freemium models: Allowing potential customers to experience the value of your product or service firsthand.

Regardless of the format, your lead magnet must be high-quality, well-designed, and offer genuine value to the subscriber. Poorly written, poorly designed, or irrelevant content will detract from your brand and hinder your list-building efforts. Invest time and resources in creating a lead magnet that meets your audience's needs and expectations. Consider employing professional writers, designers, or video editors if necessary to ensure your lead magnet is of the highest quality.

Beyond the lead magnet itself, the way you present it is crucial. Your opt-in form should be strategically placed on your website and other online platforms. Avoid burying it deep within your site; make it easily accessible and visually appealing. A prominent opt-in form on your homepage, strategically placed within your blog posts, and incorporated into your social media strategy can significantly increase your conversion rates.

Consider A/B testing different opt-in forms to optimize their performance. Experiment with variations in design, copy, and placement to determine what works best for your audience. Tools like Google Optimize or other A/B testing software can help you track the results of your experiments and make data-driven decisions.

Contests and giveaways are another powerful way to build your email list. By offering a valuable prize in exchange for an email address, you can attract a large number of subscribers quickly. However, ensure the prize is relevant to your target audience and aligned with your brand. A contest or giveaway should not only attract new subscribers but also strengthen your brand's relationship with existing customers.

To maximize the effectiveness of your contest, promote it across multiple channels, including social media, your website, and email marketing (if you already have an existing list). Ensure the entry process is simple and straightforward, minimizing the barrier to entry for potential participants. Clearly communicate the contest rules and deadlines to avoid confusion and maintain transparency. Following the contest, nurture these new leads with engaging and valuable content.

Building a successful email list necessitates a deep understanding of your target audience. This enables you to tailor your lead magnets and opt-in strategies to resonate effectively with your ideal subscribers. Conduct thorough market research to understand the needs, pain points, and preferences of your target market. Employ various market research techniques, from surveys and interviews to analyzing competitor strategies and utilizing social media analytics. These insights will guide the development of compelling lead magnets and effective opt-in strategies.

Once you've attracted subscribers, nurturing them is just as crucial as acquiring them. This involves sending them valuable and engaging content that keeps them interested and prevents unsubscribes. Segment your list based on demographics, interests, and purchasing behavior to personalize your email marketing efforts. Use data to understand the preferences of your subscribers and tailor your messaging accordingly. Employ automated email sequences to welcome new subscribers, promote new products or services, and share valuable content.

Respecting subscriber privacy is paramount. Ensure your email marketing practices comply with all relevant regulations, such as GDPR and CAN-SPAM. Clearly state your privacy policy and provide subscribers with easy access to unsubscribe from your email list. Transparency and respect for subscriber data are fundamental to building a strong and trusting relationship with your audience.

Finally, choose the right email marketing tools to support your efforts. Various email marketing platforms are available, each with its own set of features and capabilities. Consider factors such as ease of use, automation capabilities, reporting features, and integration with other marketing tools when selecting a platform. Popular choices include

Mailchimp, Constant Contact, ActiveCampaign, and ConvertKit. Each platform offers unique features and pricing plans, so choose one that aligns with your budget and business needs. Remember, the right tool can significantly streamline your email marketing efforts, increasing efficiency and effectiveness.

Building a targeted email list is an ongoing process that requires continuous refinement and improvement. Regularly analyze your email marketing metrics, such as open rates, click-through rates, and conversion rates, to identify areas for improvement. A/B test different email subject lines, content, and call-to-actions to optimize your campaigns. Continuously evaluate the effectiveness of your lead magnets and opt-in strategies to ensure they remain relevant and compelling to your target audience. By incorporating data-driven decision-making into your email marketing strategy, you can ensure your list-building efforts remain efficient and productive, ultimately driving sustainable growth for your business.

Crafting Compelling Email Content

Now that we've established the importance of building a high-quality email list, let's delve into the crucial next step: crafting compelling email content. The most meticulously built email list will yield minimal results if your emails fail to engage and resonate with your subscribers. This section focuses on creating email content that not only captures attention but also nurtures relationships and drives conversions.

The foundation of compelling email content lies in understanding your audience. Your emails shouldn't be generic blasts; they should be personalized messages tailored to the specific needs and interests of your subscribers. This requires segmenting your email list based on demographics, behavior, and preferences. For instance, you might segment your list based on purchasing history, engagement levels, or expressed interests captured through previous interactions. This allows you to deliver targeted messages that are highly relevant to each segment, maximizing engagement and minimizing unsubscribes. Imagine a clothing retailer sending a promotional email about a new line of winter coats to subscribers who have previously purchased similar items. This targeted approach is far more effective than sending a generic email promoting all new products to the entire list.

Personalization extends beyond segmentation. Using subscribers' names in the email subject line and body is a simple yet powerful way to create a more personal connection. Consider incorporating dynamic content, which automatically adjusts the email's content based on individual subscriber data. This could include product recommendations based on past purchases or personalized offers tailored to their specific interests. The key is to make each subscriber feel seen and understood, fostering a sense of loyalty and trust.

Beyond personalization, the structure and format of your email are crucial. Avoid overwhelming your subscribers with walls of text. Use clear headings, bullet points, and visuals to break up the content and make it easier to read and digest. Consider the use of white space to improve readability and visual appeal. Emails should be visually clean and easy to navigate, guiding subscribers smoothly toward your desired call to action.

Storytelling is a powerful technique for creating engaging email content. Instead of simply listing product features or announcing sales, weave a narrative that connects with your audience on an emotional level. Share customer success stories, highlight your company's mission and values, or tell the story behind your products or services. This approach helps build brand personality and create a more meaningful connection with your subscribers. For example, a coffee roaster could share the story of their farmers or the journey of their beans, connecting with subscribers on a more emotional level than simply highlighting the caffeine content.

Calls to action (CTAs) are essential elements of any effective email campaign. Your CTA should clearly tell subscribers what you want them to do next – whether it's visiting your website, making a purchase, downloading a resource, or signing up for a webinar. Avoid vague or confusing CTAs. Use strong action verbs and create a sense of urgency to encourage immediate engagement. Consider A/B testing different CTAs to determine which ones resonate best with your audience.

Email subject lines are the first impression your subscribers receive. They determine whether your email will even be opened. Craft compelling subject lines that pique your subscribers' curiosity and accurately reflect the email's content. Use strong verbs, numbers, and personalization to create intriguing subject lines. However, avoid using deceptive or misleading subject lines, which can damage your sender reputation and increase your chances of being flagged as spam. A/B test your subject lines to see which ones perform best. Analyzing open rates will highlight what resonates most with your audience.

Maintaining a consistent brand voice across all your email communications is crucial for building brand recognition and trust. Your email style should align with your overall brand personality. Whether you're aiming for a professional, playful, or sophisticated tone, consistency is key. This includes using consistent language, imagery, and design elements across your emails.

Avoiding spam filters is crucial for ensuring your emails reach your subscribers' inboxes. Avoid using excessive capitalization, excessive exclamation points, and spam trigger words. Ensure your email content adheres to all relevant email marketing regulations such as CAN-SPAM and GDPR. Maintain a clean email list, regularly removing inactive or unengaged subscribers to reduce the risk of your emails being flagged as spam. Monitor your email deliverability rates and take corrective actions as needed.

Finally, remember that email marketing is an iterative process. Regularly analyze your email marketing metrics, including open rates, click-through rates, and conversion rates, to assess the performance of your campaigns. Use this data to refine your email content, subject lines, and CTAs, ensuring that your email marketing strategy is constantly evolving and improving. By implementing these strategies and continually refining your approach based on data and feedback, you'll transform your email communications into a powerful tool for building relationships, nurturing leads, and driving business growth. Your email marketing shouldn't just be transactional; it should be a conversation, a valuable interaction that strengthens your connection with your audience and fosters lasting loyalty. This requires ongoing effort, experimentation, and a commitment to understanding and meeting your subscribers' needs. The return, however, is a strong, engaged community that forms the bedrock of your online presence and success.

Segmenting Your Email List for Targeted Campaigns

Building a robust email list is only half the battle; the real power lies in harnessing that list effectively. This involves moving beyond generic email blasts and embracing targeted campaigns tailored to specific audience segments. Segmenting your email list allows you to deliver highly relevant messages, boosting engagement, increasing conversions, and fostering stronger customer relationships. Ignoring segmentation means missing out on a crucial opportunity to optimize your email marketing efforts. Think of it like this: would you send the same marketing message to a new customer and a loyal, repeat buyer? Of course not. Their needs, interests, and purchase intentions differ significantly. Segmentation allows you to tailor your approach to each, maximizing the impact of your message.

The foundation of effective segmentation lies in understanding your data. What information do you have on your subscribers? Consider demographics like age, location, and gender. Analyze their interests, perhaps gleaned from website activity, purchase history, or survey responses. Explore their engagement level with past emails – open rates, click-through rates, and even whether they've made purchases after receiving a particular email provide valuable insights. Don't underestimate the power of purchase history. A subscriber who frequently buys organic coffee will likely be far more receptive to an email announcing a new line of organic teas than someone who predominantly purchases conventional coffee. Similarly, a customer who consistently purchases high-end items might be more interested in exclusive offers or early access to new products than a price-sensitive shopper.

This data-driven approach allows for precise segmentation, enabling the creation of highly targeted campaigns. Instead of sending a single, broad email to your entire list, you can now craft personalized messages for specific segments. For example, a skincare company might segment its list into categories based on skin type (oily, dry, combination, sensitive) and age group. This enables them to send targeted emails promoting products specifically designed for each segment. An email featuring acne-fighting products would resonate strongly with teenagers with oily skin but might be irrelevant to older subscribers with dry skin. Similarly, an email focusing on anti-aging products would appeal more to mature customers than to younger audiences.

Beyond demographics and purchase history, behavior plays a crucial role in segmentation. Track your subscribers' interactions with your website and emails. Those who frequently open and click on your emails show a higher level of engagement and interest. They represent a valuable segment ready to receive more frequent communications about new products or promotions. Conversely, subscribers who rarely interact with your emails might benefit from a less frequent communication strategy or a different approach entirely. Perhaps a more personalized outreach or a targeted email series designed to re-engage them would prove more effective. Analyzing bounce rates and unsubscribes can also help you refine your segmentation strategies. High bounce rates could suggest issues with email deliverability, while high unsubscribe rates may indicate that you're sending irrelevant content to a particular segment.

Leveraging email marketing tools is essential for effective list segmentation. Most email marketing platforms offer sophisticated segmentation capabilities, allowing you to easily create and manage various segments. These tools enable you to create segments based on multiple criteria, allowing for precise targeting. For instance, you could create a segment of subscribers who have purchased a specific product in the last month and also opened your last three emails. This highly targeted segment is ideal for promoting complementary products or offering exclusive discounts. The capabilities often include automated segmentation, allowing you to dynamically add subscribers to segments based on their actions, such as completing a purchase or downloading a resource. This ensures that your segments are always up-to-date and reflect the latest subscriber behavior.

Implementing these tools effectively requires a clear understanding of your business goals. What do you hope to achieve with your email marketing campaigns? Increased sales? Enhanced brand awareness? Lead generation? Your goals should directly inform your segmentation strategy. If your primary goal is to drive sales, you might segment your list based on purchase history and engagement level. If your goal is to nurture leads, you might segment your list based on lead source and level of engagement with your content. The key is to align your segmentation strategy with your overall business objectives.

Consider a hypothetical example of a bookstore. They could segment their email list based on genre preferences (fiction, non-fiction, mystery, romance, etc.), purchase frequency (frequent buyers, infrequent buyers, new subscribers), and specific author preferences. This enables them to send targeted recommendations: a frequent buyer of thrillers might receive an email highlighting new releases in that genre, while a new subscriber who purchased a biography might receive recommendations for similar titles. This personalized approach significantly increases the likelihood of a purchase, enhancing customer loyalty and driving sales.

Beyond simply segmenting your list, you can create highly personalized email experiences by utilizing dynamic content. This involves tailoring the content of your emails based on individual subscriber data. Imagine an email recommending specific products based on past purchases or browsing history. Or consider an email that dynamically adjusts the pricing or offers based on the subscriber's location or past interactions. These personalized touches create a stronger connection with your audience, making your emails feel less like generic marketing messages and more like valued communications.

But remember, segmentation is not a one-time task. It's an ongoing process requiring continuous monitoring and refinement. Regularly review your segmentation strategy, analyzing the performance of your campaigns and adjusting your segments as needed. New data constantly emerges, changing subscriber behavior and preferences. Tracking key metrics like open rates, click-through rates, and conversion rates will reveal which segments are most responsive to your campaigns and which need a revised approach. A/B testing different email variations within each segment allows for further optimization, ensuring you continuously refine your strategy for optimal effectiveness.

By implementing a well-defined segmentation strategy, leveraging the capabilities of email marketing tools, and continuously analyzing the results, you can transform your email marketing from a generic broadcast to a personalized conversation. This targeted approach will not only boost your campaign effectiveness but also foster stronger relationships with your subscribers, turning them into loyal customers and advocates for your brand. The key is to continually strive for relevance; emails should always feel timely, insightful, and valuable to the recipient. This dedication to personalization creates a positive feedback loop, rewarding your efforts with increased engagement, higher conversion rates, and ultimately, a thriving online presence.

Automating Your Email Marketing

Automating your email marketing isn't about replacing human connection; it's about strategically leveraging technology to enhance it. Think of automation as your tireless assistant, handling repetitive tasks so you can focus on crafting compelling content and building meaningful relationships. It frees up valuable time and resources, allowing you to scale your email marketing efforts without sacrificing personalization or effectiveness. Effective automation enables you to nurture leads, convert prospects, and cultivate long-term customer loyalty with consistent, timely communication, all while maintaining a personal touch.

The cornerstone of automated email marketing lies in defining clear goals and objectives. What do you hope to achieve? Are you aiming to boost sales, increase brand awareness, generate leads, or improve customer retention? Your goals will dictate the types of automation workflows you implement. For example, if lead generation is your primary goal, you might focus on automated welcome sequences and nurture campaigns. If sales are your priority, abandoned cart emails and post-purchase follow-ups will be crucial. A clear understanding of your objectives will ensure that your automation strategy directly supports your overarching business goals.

One of the most effective automation strategies is the welcome sequence. This series of automated emails is triggered when a new subscriber joins your email list. It serves as a crucial first impression, setting the tone for your future interactions and laying the foundation for a strong customer relationship. Avoid generic greetings; instead, craft personalized messages that showcase your brand's personality and offer valuable content relevant to your subscribers' interests. A welcome sequence might include an introductory email thanking subscribers for joining, an email highlighting your brand story and values, and an email offering a valuable lead magnet, such as an ebook, discount code, or exclusive content. This sequence should be designed to nurture new subscribers and establish them as valuable members of your community.

Beyond welcome sequences, abandoned cart emails are a powerful tool for recovering lost sales. These automated emails are triggered when a customer adds items to their shopping cart but fails to complete the purchase. These emails offer a gentle reminder and often include incentives, such as free shipping or a discount, to encourage the customer to finalize their purchase. A well-crafted abandoned cart email can significantly boost conversion rates, turning potential lost sales into revenue. It's not just about simply reminding them; it's about understanding the potential reasons for cart abandonment. Was the shipping cost too high? Was there a lack of payment options? Addressing these concerns in your email can increase your chances of recovery.

Post-purchase follow-up sequences are equally important for cultivating customer loyalty and driving repeat business. These automated emails are triggered after a customer makes a purchase. They often include thank-you messages, product recommendations, or helpful tips related to the purchased item. This thoughtful communication reinforces the customer's decision and enhances their overall shopping experience. Post-purchase follow-ups can also be used to collect feedback or encourage product reviews, providing valuable insight into customer satisfaction and product performance. It's a chance to turn a one-time customer into a loyal advocate for your brand.

Beyond these core automation strategies, there's a wide range of possibilities depending on your industry and specific business needs. Consider automated birthday emails to personalize the customer experience. Or perhaps automated email campaigns to promote seasonal sales or special events. These targeted promotions create anticipation and excitement, increasing engagement and driving sales. Automated feedback requests can help you improve your products and services, while win-back campaigns can help re-engage inactive customers, preventing churn.

Choosing the right email automation tools is crucial for success. Several platforms offer robust automation capabilities, catering to different business needs and budgets. Some platforms are ideal for small businesses with limited resources, offering intuitive interfaces and basic automation features. Others are designed for larger enterprises, offering more advanced features and scalability. When selecting a platform, consider your budget, the size of your email list, the complexity of your automation needs, and the level of integration with your existing marketing tools. Key features to look for include easy-to-use workflows, segmentation capabilities, A/B testing functionalities, and reporting and analytics dashboards.

Implementation and optimization are ongoing processes. Once your automation workflows are set up, it's essential to monitor their performance and make adjustments as needed. Track key metrics such as open rates, click-through rates, conversion rates, and unsubscribe rates. Analyze the data to identify areas for improvement, such as refining your email content, adjusting your segmentation strategies, or optimizing your workflow triggers. Regular A/B testing of email variations can help you identify what resonates most effectively with your audience. Remember, automation is not a "set it and forget it" process; continuous monitoring and optimization are key to achieving optimal results.

Let's consider some specific examples. A clothing retailer might use automation to send abandoned cart emails, post-purchase follow-ups with styling tips, and personalized product recommendations based on past purchases. An educational institution could use automation to send welcome emails to new students, course reminders, and graduation announcements. A software company might automate onboarding emails for new users, product updates, and training materials. These examples highlight the versatility of email automation and its applicability across diverse industries.

In the context of a bookstore, automation can personalize the customer journey significantly. A welcome sequence could introduce the bookstore's unique features, such as author events or book clubs. Abandoned cart emails could remind customers about books left in their cart, suggesting similar titles based on their previous browsing history. Post-purchase follow-ups could offer recommendations based on the customer's recent purchase, encouraging further engagement with the bookstore's offerings. Personalized birthday emails could offer a discount on a book selected based on the customer's preferred genres. These automated communications make the customer feel valued and appreciated, fostering brand loyalty and driving repeat business.

Remember, successful email automation isn't about bombarding subscribers with emails; it's about providing value and building relationships. Always prioritize quality over quantity. Focus on crafting engaging, relevant content that resonates with your audience. Avoid generic, mass-produced emails. Personalize your messages as much as possible, using subscriber data to tailor the content to their specific interests. By carefully implementing automation and continuously analyzing your results, you can transform your email marketing strategy from a sporadic effort to a powerful engine for growth and customer engagement. The goal is to create a seamless, personalized experience that strengthens your connection with your audience and drives meaningful results. Automation is the key to unlocking the full potential of your email marketing, turning it into a highly efficient and effective tool for achieving your business objectives.

Measuring Email Marketing Results and ROI

Measuring the success of your email marketing efforts isn't simply about sending out emails and hoping for the best. It requires a strategic approach to tracking key performance indicators (KPIs) and meticulously analyzing the data to understand what works and what doesn't. This allows for data-driven decisions that optimize your campaigns and maximize your return on investment (ROI). Ignoring this crucial aspect is like navigating a ship without a compass – you might reach your destination eventually, but the journey will be far more arduous, costly, and potentially unsuccessful.

The foundation of effective email marketing measurement lies in defining clear, measurable goals. Before launching any campaign, articulate what you want to achieve. Are you aiming to increase brand awareness, drive traffic to your website, generate leads, boost sales, or improve customer retention? Each goal necessitates specific metrics to track and analyze. For example, if your objective is lead generation, you'll focus on metrics like click-through rates (CTRs) on lead magnets and form submissions. If your goal is boosting sales, conversion rates and revenue generated from email campaigns become paramount. Without these well-defined goals, your data analysis becomes a meaningless exercise.

Let's delve into some of the crucial metrics you should consistently monitor:

Open Rates: This metric indicates the percentage of recipients who opened your email. A low open rate might signal issues with your subject line, sender reputation, or the time of day you're sending emails. Analyzing trends in open rates over time can reveal patterns and highlight areas for improvement. A/B testing different subject lines is crucial for identifying what resonates best with your audience.

Click-Through Rates (CTRs): CTR measures the percentage of recipients who clicked on a link within your email. This metric reflects the effectiveness of your email's content and call to action (CTA). A low CTR could indicate that your email content isn't engaging enough or that your CTA isn't clear or compelling. Testing different CTAs and refining your email content based on data analysis can significantly improve CTRs.

Conversion Rates: This is perhaps the most critical metric, reflecting the percentage of recipients who completed a desired action after clicking a link in your email. This action could be making a purchase, filling out a form, signing up for a trial, or downloading a resource. A low conversion rate may suggest issues with your landing page, website design, or the overall user experience.

Unsubscribe Rates: While not a desirable metric, a high unsubscribe rate provides valuable insights into areas of dissatisfaction among your subscribers. A significant increase in unsubscribes may signal that your emails are irrelevant, too frequent, or simply not engaging. Analyzing the reasons behind unsubscribes, often through surveys or feedback mechanisms, can help you understand and address the concerns of your audience.

Bounce Rates: Bounce rates measure the percentage of emails that were not delivered to the recipient's inbox. High bounce rates can indicate problems with your email list hygiene, such as invalid email addresses or full inboxes. Regularly cleaning your email list and employing techniques to validate email addresses are essential to maintaining a healthy list and reducing bounce rates.

Beyond these core metrics, you can track more granular data depending on your campaign objectives. For instance, you might track social media shares, time spent on your website after clicking an email link, or the number of customer support requests generated by email interactions.

To effectively measure these metrics, you need robust email marketing analytics and reporting tools. Most email marketing platforms provide comprehensive dashboards and reports that track these KPIs. These dashboards offer a visual representation of your campaign performance, allowing you to easily identify trends and areas for improvement. Look for platforms that provide detailed segmentation capabilities, allowing you to analyze the performance of your campaigns across different subscriber groups.

Data-driven decision-making is essential for optimizing email marketing campaigns. Regularly analyzing your data allows you to identify what's working and what's not. If your open rates are consistently low, experiment with different subject lines and send times. If your CTRs are poor, revise your email content and CTA. If your conversion rates are lagging, investigate potential issues with your website or landing pages. A/B testing different elements of your email campaigns, such as subject lines, content, and CTAs, allows for a scientific approach to optimization.

Remember, continuous monitoring and optimization are ongoing processes. Email marketing is not a "set it and forget it" strategy. Regularly reviewing your campaign performance, analyzing your data, and making data-driven adjustments are crucial for maximizing your ROI. Treat your email marketing data as a valuable resource, a compass guiding you towards more effective and efficient campaigns.

Let's consider a practical example. Suppose a small online bookstore is running an email campaign to promote a new release. They'll track open rates to assess the effectiveness of their subject line. Then, they'll monitor CTRs to see how many recipients clicked on the link to the book's page. Furthermore, conversion rates will reveal how many recipients ultimately purchased the book. Analyzing these metrics can provide insights into the campaign's strengths and weaknesses. For example, if the open rates are low, they might revise their subject line. If the CTRs are low, they might improve the visual appeal of the email or make the CTA more prominent. If the conversion rates are low, they might review their website design or the pricing strategy for the book.

This iterative process of monitoring, analyzing, and optimizing is fundamental to achieving sustained growth in your email marketing endeavors. Don't underestimate the power of data-driven decisions. The insights you gain from meticulously tracking your KPIs can dramatically improve your campaign performance and, ultimately, your overall ROI. The key lies in consistently refining your strategy based on real-world data, ensuring your email marketing efforts are not only efficient but also highly effective in achieving your business objectives. By embracing this continuous improvement approach, you'll transform your email marketing from a potentially inefficient expense into a powerful revenue-generating engine. Remember, the ultimate goal is to build lasting relationships with your customers, nurture their engagement, and translate that engagement into tangible business results, all while efficiently allocating your marketing resources.

Identifying Content Gaps and Opportunities

Understanding your audience's needs and desires is paramount to successful content marketing. Simply creating content for the sake of it won't cut it. You need to strategically identify gaps and opportunities within the existing content landscape to create material that truly resonates and provides value to your target audience. This involves a multifaceted approach that combines meticulous keyword research, thorough competitive analysis, and insightful audience feedback analysis. Let's delve into each of these crucial components.

Keyword Research: Unearthing Hidden Gems

Keyword research forms the bedrock of effective content strategy. It's about identifying the specific terms and phrases your target audience uses when searching for information online. This isn't simply about finding high-volume keywords; it's about understanding the intent behind those searches. Are users looking for information, products, or solutions? Understanding this intent allows you to create content that directly addresses their needs.

Several tools can assist in this process. Google Keyword Planner, a free tool within Google Ads, provides insights into search volume, competition, and related keywords. SEMrush and Ahrefs are more advanced tools offering a broader range of features, including keyword difficulty scores, competitive analysis, and backlink analysis. These tools allow you to delve deeper into the search landscape and identify keywords with lower competition but significant search volume – representing valuable opportunities to create content that ranks well organically.

Beyond these tools, exploring forums, social media groups, and online communities relevant to your industry provides invaluable insights into the language your target audience uses. Observe the questions they ask, the problems they face, and the information they seek. This qualitative research complements the quantitative data provided by keyword research tools, enriching your understanding of the topics your audience cares about.

For example, if you're a company specializing in sustainable fashion, a simple keyword search might reveal high-volume terms like "sustainable clothing" or "eco-friendly fashion." However, digging deeper using tools like Ahrefs or SEMrush might unveil long-tail keywords like "best sustainable dresses for petite women" or "how to care for organic cotton clothing." These longer, more specific keywords represent niche opportunities to create highly targeted content that addresses specific audience segments, ultimately leading to greater engagement and conversion rates.

Furthermore, don't overlook the power of question-based keywords. Tools like AnswerThePublic provide a visual representation of questions people ask related to a specific topic. This can inspire content ideas such as blog posts, FAQs, or video tutorials addressing these specific questions. By anticipating and answering your audience's questions, you establish yourself as a trusted resource and cultivate a loyal following.

Competitive Analysis: Learning from the Best (and the Rest)

Competitive analysis goes beyond simply observing what your competitors are doing. It's about identifying content gaps, understanding their strengths and weaknesses, and discovering untapped opportunities. Analyzing your competitors' websites, blogs, and social media presence can reveal areas where they are lacking and opportunities for you to excel.

Look at the type of content they are creating, the keywords they are targeting, and their overall content strategy. Are they neglecting certain topics or focusing too heavily on others? Are there opportunities to create more comprehensive, in-depth content than what's currently available? This analysis helps you differentiate your content and establish your brand as a leader in your industry.

For instance, let's say you're a digital marketing agency. Analyzing your competitors' blogs might reveal that they predominantly focus on SEO and social media marketing, but are neglecting content marketing strategies. This represents a gap in the market—an opportunity for you to create high-quality, comprehensive content on this under-served area, establishing your expertise and attracting potential clients seeking comprehensive marketing services.

Utilizing tools like SEMrush or Ahrefs can automate much of this analysis. These tools allow you to compare your website's performance with your competitors' on various metrics, including keyword rankings, backlink profiles, and overall website traffic. This comparative analysis provides valuable insights into areas for improvement and untapped opportunities.

Remember, competitive analysis isn't about copying your competitors. It's about identifying their shortcomings and using that information to inform your content strategy, creating something better, more comprehensive, and more valuable to your target audience.

Audience Feedback Analysis: Listening to the Voice of the Customer

Directly engaging with your audience is essential for understanding their needs and identifying content opportunities. Collecting feedback through surveys, polls, social media engagement, and comments on your existing content provides invaluable insights into what resonates with your audience and where there's room for improvement.

Analyzing comments on your blog posts, social media updates, and other online platforms reveals which topics generate the most engagement and which ones are ignored. This helps you identify areas where you can create more valuable content. Similarly, conducting surveys or polls allows you to directly ask your audience about their needs and preferences. This data provides direct, actionable insights that you can use to refine your content strategy and create material that truly resonates.

Consider incorporating feedback mechanisms directly into your content. For example, include a poll at the end of a blog post to gauge your audience's preferences or ask a direct question in your social media posts to stimulate interaction and gather valuable data.

Utilizing social listening tools can also prove beneficial. These tools analyze social media conversations and identify mentions of your brand or industry-related topics. This helps you understand what people are saying about you and your competitors, allowing you to address concerns, identify content gaps, and create content that directly addresses these conversations.

For example, if you're a food blogger and consistently receive comments asking for vegan recipes, this indicates a clear content gap. Creating a series of vegan recipes directly responds to this audience demand, potentially leading to increased engagement and a larger audience.

By actively listening to your audience, you demonstrate that you value their opinions, fostering a sense of community and loyalty. Furthermore, this feedback forms the foundation of a data-driven content strategy, ensuring that you're creating content that meets the actual needs and desires of your target audience.

Integrating Your Findings and Selecting Winning Topics

Once you've conducted keyword research, competitive analysis, and audience feedback analysis, it's time to integrate your findings and select winning topics. Prioritize topics that align with your business goals, target audience needs, and identified content gaps.

Consider creating a content calendar to plan and schedule your content creation. This allows for a structured and organized approach, ensuring consistent content delivery. Remember to prioritize quality over quantity; a few high-quality pieces of content are far more effective than a large volume of low-quality content. Focus on creating content that is valuable, informative, and engaging. Utilize a variety of formats, including blog posts, videos, infographics, and podcasts, to cater to the preferences of your target audience.

Regularly review and update your content strategy based on your performance data. Track your content's performance using analytics tools to identify what's working and what's not. This continuous improvement process is crucial for maintaining a relevant and engaging content strategy.

Remember, content marketing is a marathon, not a sprint. Consistency, quality, and audience engagement are crucial for long-term success. By following these steps and consistently refining your strategy, you can create content that resonates with your target audience, attracts new customers, and ultimately drives business growth. The key lies in understanding your audience, recognizing the gaps in the market, and creating valuable content that fills those gaps and establishes your brand as a leader in your industry.

Creating HighQuality Engaging Content

Creating compelling content is the lifeblood of any successful content marketing strategy. It's not enough to simply churn out words; you need to craft engaging narratives that resonate with your audience, providing value and leaving a lasting impression. This requires a multifaceted approach encompassing diverse content formats, strategic storytelling, and meticulous optimization for different platforms. Let's delve into the specifics.

First, consider the power of storytelling. Humans are inherently drawn to narratives. A well-crafted story can evoke emotions, build connections, and make your brand memorable. Instead of simply stating facts, weave them into a compelling narrative that engages your audience on an emotional level. Think about the structure of your story: establish a relatable problem, present a solution, and offer a satisfying resolution. This approach makes information more palatable and memorable, increasing the likelihood of your audience retaining and sharing your message. For instance, a company selling sustainable cleaning products could tell the story of the founder's journey towards eco-consciousness, highlighting the environmental impact of traditional cleaning products and the benefits of switching to sustainable alternatives. This personal touch humanizes the brand and makes the product message more relatable.

Next, recognize the diverse formats available for content creation. While blog posts and articles remain cornerstones of content marketing, exploring other formats expands your reach and caters to diverse audience preferences. Infographics transform complex data into visually appealing and easily digestible content, ideal for conveying statistics or key findings. Videos are incredibly versatile, from short explainer videos to longer documentary-style pieces. Podcasts offer an intimate listening experience, perfect for in-depth discussions or interviews. Each format presents unique opportunities to engage your audience in different ways. For example, a financial advisory firm could use infographics to explain complex investment strategies, create short videos answering frequently asked questions, and host a podcast featuring interviews with successful investors. This multi-format approach ensures your message reaches a wider audience, catering to various consumption preferences.

Optimizing content for different platforms is crucial for maximizing reach and engagement. A blog post optimized for Google search may not perform well on social media. Understanding the nuances of each platform is essential. For instance, social media posts require concise, attention-grabbing content with compelling visuals. Similarly, optimizing blog posts for search engines involves thorough keyword research, meta descriptions, and internal linking. Video content requires attention-grabbing thumbnails and titles optimized for discoverability on platforms like YouTube. Podcast optimization involves selecting a clear title and descriptive show notes to improve visibility on podcast directories. This targeted approach ensures your content resonates with the specific audience on each platform.

Providing genuine value is paramount to successful content marketing. Avoid creating content solely for self-promotion; focus on offering information that is useful, informative, and entertaining to your audience. This could include providing practical tips, answering frequently asked questions, offering tutorials, or sharing insightful perspectives on industry trends. Think about the problems your audience faces and create content that directly addresses those issues. For instance, a software company could create tutorials demonstrating how to use their software efficiently, addressing common user challenges. A travel agency could create blog posts offering tips for planning budget-friendly trips or choosing the best travel insurance. By focusing on providing value, you build trust with your audience, positioning your brand as a helpful resource and fostering long-term engagement.

Furthermore, ensuring the quality of your content is paramount. Poorly written, poorly researched, or visually unappealing content can damage your brand reputation and deter potential customers. Invest time in ensuring that your content is accurate, well-written, and visually appealing. Use high-quality images, videos, and graphics to enhance the visual appeal of your content. Proofread your work carefully to avoid errors and typos. Employ a consistent brand voice and tone across all your content to ensure a cohesive brand identity. Seek feedback from others before publishing to identify areas for improvement. Consider engaging professional editors or designers to ensure the highest level of quality. The investment in quality content far outweighs the cost of creating substandard content that may negatively impact your brand.

Consider repurposing existing content to maximize its impact and extend its reach. A blog post can be transformed into a series of social media posts, an infographic, or a short video. A podcast episode can be transcribed into a blog post or a series of tweets. This strategy extends the lifespan of your content and increases its exposure to a broader audience. Repurposing also ensures you're maximizing the return on investment of your content creation efforts. For example, a successful webinar can be edited into a series of short, shareable video clips for social media platforms. The key is to adapt the content to fit the specific format and audience of each platform, ensuring the message remains relevant and engaging.

Remember that consistent content creation is crucial for maintaining engagement and building a loyal audience. Develop a content calendar to plan and schedule your content creation efforts. This ensures a regular flow of fresh, relevant content that keeps your audience engaged. Regularly review and analyze your content performance using analytics tools such as Google Analytics. This data helps you identify what is working and what isn't, enabling you to refine your content strategy and optimize your efforts. Continuously adjust your content strategy based on data, feedback, and emerging trends. The ever-evolving digital landscape requires flexibility and adaptability. What works today may not work tomorrow; continuous monitoring and adjustment are essential for long-term success.

Finally, integrate your content across all your marketing channels to maximize its impact. Share your blog posts on social media, embed your videos on your website, and promote your podcasts on your email list. This cross-promotion strategy expands the reach of your content and ensures that your audience has multiple opportunities to engage with it. For instance, a company launching a new product could create a blog post explaining the product's features, share it on social media, and include it in their email newsletter. This multi-pronged approach increases the likelihood that your message will reach your target audience. By seamlessly weaving your content across various channels, you amplify its impact and build a stronger, more cohesive brand presence. The ultimate goal is not only to create high-quality content but also to distribute it effectively, ensuring maximum reach and engagement. A well-executed content strategy is an investment in your brand's future, and the rewards of carefully curated content will far outweigh the initial effort.

Content Promotion and Distribution

The creation of compelling content is only half the battle; effective distribution is equally crucial. A masterpiece languishing unseen is a missed opportunity. This section focuses on amplifying your content's reach through strategic promotion and distribution across diverse channels. The key lies in a multi-channel approach, understanding the nuances of each platform, and optimizing your content to resonate with the specific audience on each.

Social media offers a powerful platform for content promotion. However, simply posting your content and hoping for the best is rarely sufficient. A strategic approach requires understanding your target audience's social media habits. Are they primarily on Facebook, Instagram, Twitter, LinkedIn, or TikTok? The platform choice directly impacts your content strategy. A visually driven platform like Instagram demands high-quality images and short, attention-grabbing captions. LinkedIn, on the other hand, benefits from more in-depth, professionally oriented content.

Consider the timing of your posts. Social media algorithms favor engagement, so scheduling posts during peak activity hours can significantly enhance visibility. Utilize analytics tools provided by each platform to identify optimal posting times for your target audience. Beyond simple posting, engage with your audience. Respond to comments and questions promptly, fostering a sense of community and building relationships. Run contests or giveaways to increase engagement and brand awareness. Collaborate with influencers in your niche to expand your reach to a wider audience. Their established following can bring fresh eyes to your content, particularly effective for smaller businesses lacking a significant organic reach.

Email marketing remains a highly effective tool for content promotion, offering a direct line of communication with your audience. Building a loyal email list requires providing genuine value in exchange for email addresses – perhaps offering a lead magnet like an ebook or checklist. Once you have a list, segment your audience based on interests or behaviors to personalize your email communications. Avoid generic blasts; tailor your emails to the specific segments, ensuring the content aligns with their interests. Employ a compelling subject line that piques interest and encourages recipients to open the email. Use a clear and concise email body that highlights the value proposition of your content. Include a clear call to action, directing recipients to your website or a specific landing page. Regularly monitor email open and click-through rates to assess the effectiveness of your email campaigns and refine your strategy accordingly.

Paid advertising, while involving monetary investment, offers a rapid route to increased visibility. Platforms like Google Ads and social media advertising allow you to target specific demographics, interests, and behaviors, ensuring your content reaches the most relevant audience. Invest time in keyword research and audience targeting to maximize your return on investment. Experiment with different ad formats and targeting options to identify what resonates best with your audience. Carefully track your campaign performance using analytics tools to identify areas for improvement and optimize your spending. Remember that paid advertising complements, rather than replaces, organic efforts. It should be part of a holistic content marketing strategy.

Beyond these primary channels, explore other avenues for content promotion. Consider guest blogging on relevant websites or participating in industry podcasts. This increases your visibility within your niche and exposes your content to a new audience. Submitting your content to relevant directories and online communities can also expand your reach. Harness the power of social bookmarking sites, sharing your content on platforms like Pinterest and Reddit, leveraging the communities and engagement found on those platforms. Remember that consistent effort across various platforms is essential for long-term success.

Optimizing content for various platforms demands a tailored approach. A blog post optimized for search engines may require significant changes to be effective on social media. The ideal length, format, and style will vary based on the platform and audience. Google prioritizes comprehensive, high-quality content with relevant keywords, while Twitter favors brevity and impactful visuals. Facebook rewards engaging content that sparks conversations, whereas Instagram focuses on high-quality images and videos. Understanding these platform-specific requirements allows you to craft content that maximises engagement on each.

Measuring the success of your content promotion efforts is vital. Utilize analytics tools to track key metrics such as website traffic, social media engagement, email open rates, and click-through rates. Analyze this data to understand what's working and what isn't, allowing for data-driven adjustments to your strategy. Track the source of your website traffic, identifying which channels are generating the most leads and conversions. Monitor your social media analytics to measure engagement levels, identifying top-performing content and adjusting your strategy accordingly. This ongoing analysis is crucial for continuous improvement and maximizing the return on your content marketing investment. Adaptability is key; the digital landscape is constantly evolving. Regularly review your strategy and make necessary adjustments to remain effective and relevant.

In conclusion, successful content promotion requires a multi-faceted approach, combining organic and paid strategies across various channels. By understanding the strengths of each platform, optimizing your content accordingly, and consistently monitoring performance metrics, you can effectively distribute your content, amplify your reach, and achieve your marketing objectives. Remember that consistent, high-quality content remains the foundation of a thriving online presence, but without effective distribution, your efforts will fall short of their potential. The key is not only creating valuable content, but ensuring the right people see it, at the right time, on the right platform.

Measuring Content Marketing Performance

Measuring the success of your content marketing endeavors isn't simply about creating engaging content; it's about understanding how that content performs and adapting your strategy accordingly. Effective measurement requires a robust analytics framework, allowing you to track key metrics and glean actionable insights. This section delves into the crucial aspects of monitoring and interpreting content marketing performance, focusing on data-driven decision-making for optimization and improved results.

One of the most fundamental metrics is website traffic. Tools like Google Analytics provide a wealth of information, allowing you to track the number of visitors to your website, their source, their behavior on your site, and ultimately, their conversion rate. Understanding where your traffic originates – organic search, social media, email marketing, or paid advertising – allows you to pinpoint the most effective channels. For example, if a significant portion of your website traffic is driven by social media, you might allocate more resources to that channel. Conversely, if email marketing proves less effective, you may need to refine your email strategy, including subject lines, email content, and call-to-actions. Analyzing bounce rate, time on site, and pages per visit provides insights into user engagement. A high bounce rate could indicate issues with content relevance or website usability, prompting a review of your content's quality and your website's design and navigation.

Beyond website traffic, social media engagement is a crucial indicator of content success. Each social media platform offers its own analytics dashboard, providing valuable data on metrics such as likes, shares, comments, and reach.

Analyzing these metrics reveals which types of content resonate most with your audience on each platform. A post with high engagement indicates a successful piece of content, worthy of replication or expansion upon. Conversely, low engagement might suggest the need to experiment with different content formats, styles, or topics. Consider A/B testing different post types, using different visual styles, or altering the content's angle. The ability to track social media analytics enables you to tailor your content to each platform's unique audience and algorithm. For instance, a video might perform exceptionally well on Instagram but poorly on LinkedIn, highlighting the importance of platform-specific content optimization.

Lead generation is another key performance indicator (KPI) within content marketing. This involves tracking the number of potential customers who express interest in your products or services through various actions such as filling out forms, downloading resources, or signing up for newsletters. This data reveals the effectiveness of your content in attracting and nurturing potential leads. Analyzing the source of your leads provides insight into which content assets are most effective in driving conversions. For example, a blog post offering a free checklist might generate significantly more leads than a general informational blog post. This data is invaluable when allocating resources, for example, if a particular e-book download consistently generates a high number of qualified leads, investing more in similar content is justified.

Conversion rates, representing the percentage of leads who ultimately become customers, are perhaps the most crucial metric in content marketing. Tracking this metric indicates the effectiveness of your overall content strategy in driving sales or achieving desired outcomes. A low conversion rate might signal the need to improve your calls to action

(CTAs), optimize your sales funnels, or refine your targeting. Understanding which content is most effective at leading potential clients to conversion points can significantly improve your return on investment. For instance, case studies demonstrating tangible results often prove highly effective at increasing conversion rates, while white papers offer an in-depth resource that persuades potential clients.

Effective content marketing analytics goes beyond simply collecting data; it involves analyzing and interpreting the data to make informed decisions. Regular reporting, summarizing key performance indicators, allows for a comprehensive overview of the campaign's effectiveness. This report should include a comparison of past performance with current results, highlighting trends and patterns. Visual representations, like charts and graphs, effectively communicate this complex data in a clear and concise manner. This allows for easy identification of successes and areas for improvement, making it easier for stakeholders to understand progress and ROI.

To ensure the accuracy and effectiveness of your analytics, establish a clear measurement framework from the outset. Define your key performance indicators (KPIs) aligned with your overall marketing goals. These KPIs should be specific, measurable, achievable, relevant, and time-bound (SMART). For example, instead of simply aiming to "increase brand awareness," a SMART goal might be "increase brand awareness by 20% within six months, measured by social media engagement and website traffic." This ensures you're tracking the right metrics and making meaningful progress toward your overall business objectives.

Making data-driven decisions is crucial for optimizing content strategies. Regularly review your analytics dashboards, identify trends, and adapt your strategy accordingly. If a particular type of content underperforms, experiment with different formats or approaches. If a specific channel proves highly effective, allocate more resources to that channel. This iterative process of testing, analyzing, and refining your strategy is essential for maximizing the return on your content marketing investment. Moreover, this flexible approach allows you to remain adaptable in the ever-changing digital landscape. A rigid strategy that doesn't adjust to the evolving needs of the audience and the platform changes is likely to fail.

Setting realistic expectations is critical. Content marketing is a long-term strategy, not a quick fix. Don't expect overnight results; rather, focus on building a consistent, high-quality content pipeline that delivers value to your target audience. Consistent effort across various channels is vital for long-term success; a sustained approach will generate better results than a short burst of activity. Equally crucial is long-term planning, identifying your objectives, target audiences, and strategies well in advance, thereby ensuring that the content created directly contributes towards your wider marketing objectives. Without a long-term vision, you risk creating isolated pieces of content without the cohesion needed for successful campaigning.

In conclusion, measuring content marketing performance is an ongoing process requiring a holistic approach encompassing website analytics, social media engagement, lead generation, conversion rates, and data-driven decision-making. By diligently tracking key metrics, regularly reviewing your data, and adapting your strategy accordingly, you can ensure your content marketing efforts are efficient, effective, and aligned with your overall business objectives. Remember that success hinges on understanding your audience, setting realistic goals, and committing to a long-term strategy that prioritizes quality and consistent effort. By fostering this iterative approach, you are better placed to maximize the ROI of your content marketing investment and achieve sustainable growth.

Repurposing Content for Maximum Impact

Repurposing your existing content is a highly effective strategy to maximize its value and reach. Instead of viewing each piece of content as a one-off creation, consider it as a foundation upon which you can build multiple variations, extending its lifespan and broadening its audience. This approach not only saves you time and resources but also ensures that your message resonates with a wider segment of your target market across diverse platforms.

One of the most common and effective methods of content repurposing is transforming blog posts into other formats. A well-written blog post, for instance, contains a wealth of information that can be easily adapted into different media. Consider a comprehensive blog post detailing the benefits of a particular product or service. This detailed information can be transformed into a visually appealing infographic, perfect for sharing on platforms like Pinterest and Instagram, where visual content reigns supreme. The infographic, summarizing the key benefits in a concise and easily digestible format, can attract a new audience who may not be inclined to read a lengthy blog post.

Further extending the reach of this initial blog post, consider creating a short, engaging video summarizing its key points. Videos are incredibly effective at capturing attention and are highly shareable across social media platforms like YouTube, Facebook, and TikTok. The video could feature a quick overview of the product benefits, interspersed with relevant visuals and perhaps even client testimonials. This approach allows you to engage audiences who prefer visual learning or shorter content formats. By creating a concise video, you're tapping into different viewer preferences and significantly expanding the potential reach of your original blog post.

Moreover, the blog post can be easily broken down into several shorter social media posts. Each post could focus on a specific benefit or aspect of the product or service, using compelling visuals and strong calls to action. This allows you to engage your audience on platforms like Twitter, LinkedIn, and Facebook, tailoring the message to the specific platform's nuances and audience preferences. For example, a LinkedIn post might focus on the professional benefits of the product, while a Facebook post might highlight its user-friendliness. This segmented approach, born from one initial blog post, helps you optimize your message for diverse audiences.

Another effective repurposing technique involves turning case studies into presentations or webinars. Case studies, which showcase the tangible results of your products or services, are powerful tools for demonstrating value and building credibility. These detailed accounts can be transformed into presentations for conferences or internal training sessions, expanding their reach beyond a simple online publication. The data presented in a case study can also serve as the basis for an informative webinar, offering a more interactive and engaging learning experience for potential customers. This approach allows you to cultivate stronger relationships with potential leads and nurture them through the sales funnel.

Consider also transforming long-form content into short, easily digestible snippets. This is particularly relevant for platforms like Twitter and Instagram, where brevity is key. A lengthy white paper on a complex topic, for example, can be divided into multiple tweets or Instagram captions, each focusing on a specific aspect or key finding. This approach allows you to engage your audience with bite-sized pieces of valuable information, increasing the likelihood of engagement and driving traffic back to the original long-form content. Remember to include a clear call to action in each snippet, encouraging users to learn more by clicking a link to the full white paper.

Beyond these examples, there are numerous other opportunities for content repurposing. Blog posts can be adapted into podcasts, interviews, or even email newsletters. Infographics can be used as supporting material for presentations or social media campaigns. Webinars can be recorded and repurposed as video content for your website or YouTube channel. The possibilities are almost limitless, contingent only upon your creativity and the resources available. The key is to identify the core message and adapt its presentation to suit the requirements of each platform.

When repurposing content, it's crucial to adapt it to the specific platform and audience. A blog post optimized for search engines might require significant modification to be engaging on Instagram. The tone, style, and length of content should be adjusted to fit the platform's conventions and the audience's preferences. A highly technical blog post, for example, may need to be simplified significantly for a general audience on Facebook. Alternatively, content designed for a younger audience on TikTok might require a different approach than that suitable for a professional audience on LinkedIn.

Analyzing the performance of your repurposed content is just as important as the repurposing process itself. By closely monitoring key metrics such as engagement, reach, and lead generation, you can gain valuable insights into what works and what doesn't. This data-driven approach allows you to refine your repurposing strategy, maximizing the efficiency and effectiveness of your efforts. By tracking the results of your various content formats, you can identify which adaptations generate the most significant impact and tailor future repurposing efforts accordingly. This iterative process ensures that your resources are utilized effectively, maximizing your return on investment.

The success of content repurposing hinges on strategic planning and a clear understanding of your target audience. Before embarking on repurposing efforts, identify which content assets are best suited for adaptation, considering both their potential reach and their alignment with your overall marketing goals. A well-defined strategy, specifying target platforms and desired outcomes, is crucial for achieving meaningful results. Without a clear plan, you risk diluting your message and wasting valuable resources on ineffective efforts.

To illustrate successful content repurposing, let's examine a case study. A technology company released a detailed white paper on a complex software update. This paper, while comprehensive, was not widely read. Recognizing this, they repurposed the white paper's content into a series of short explainer videos, targeted towards different user segments. These videos were uploaded to YouTube and promoted on social media platforms. This adaptation resulted in a significant increase in engagement and website traffic, demonstrating the power of repurposing content to reach a broader audience.

In another example, a food blogger repurposed their popular blog recipes into visually appealing Instagram stories. These stories featured short videos demonstrating the cooking process, accompanied by attractive visuals and engaging music. This strategy dramatically increased their social media following and drove traffic to their blog, showcasing how adapting content to different platforms can enhance its reach and impact.

In conclusion, repurposing content is a cost-effective and highly efficient strategy for maximizing the reach and impact of your marketing efforts. By strategically transforming existing content into various formats and adapting it to different platforms, you can significantly expand your audience, strengthen brand awareness, and drive meaningful results. This approach not only saves you time and resources but also ensures that your message resonates with a wider range of potential customers. The key to success lies in careful planning, data-driven decision-making, and a commitment to continuous optimization. By embracing content repurposing as a core component of your marketing strategy, you are setting yourself up for sustainable growth and success.

Understanding Different Paid Advertising Channels

Paid advertising represents a powerful tool in the digital marketer's arsenal, offering the potential for rapid and targeted reach. However, navigating the diverse landscape of available channels requires a strategic approach, understanding their unique strengths and weaknesses to align them with your specific business objectives. This section will delve into several key paid advertising channels, providing a comprehensive overview to help you make informed decisions.

One of the most established and widely used platforms is Google Ads, formerly known as Google AdWords. Google Ads operates on a pay-per-click (PPC) model, meaning you only pay when a user clicks on your advertisement. This targeted advertising system allows you to reach potential customers actively searching for products or services related to your business. Through meticulous keyword research and strategic bidding, you can position your ads prominently within Google's search results pages (SERPs) and across its vast network of partner websites. The granular control offered by Google Ads allows you to specify your target audience based on demographics, location, interests, and even specific search terms. This ensures your message reaches the most receptive audience, maximizing your return on investment (ROI). Furthermore, Google Ads provides extensive tracking and reporting capabilities, enabling you to monitor campaign performance in real-time and make data-driven adjustments to optimize your results. This continuous optimization process is crucial for maximizing the effectiveness of your Google Ads campaigns.

However, the effectiveness of Google Ads relies heavily on the expertise of the advertiser. Competitive bidding can drive up costs, especially for highly sought-after keywords. Crafting compelling ad copy that resonates with the target audience and accurately reflects the offered product or service is paramount. Poorly designed campaigns can result in wasted ad spend and minimal returns. A successful Google Ads campaign requires thorough keyword research, compelling ad copy, precise targeting, and continuous monitoring and optimization. This necessitates either significant in-house expertise or the engagement of a skilled Google Ads specialist.

Social media advertising provides another avenue for reaching potential customers, leveraging the massive reach and engagement of platforms like Facebook, Instagram, Twitter, LinkedIn, and TikTok. Each platform boasts a unique user demographic and engagement style, requiring a tailored approach to advertising. Facebook and Instagram, for example, are ideal for visually driven campaigns, utilizing compelling imagery and video content to capture attention. LinkedIn, on the other hand, is more suitable for professional networking and B2B marketing, offering targeted advertising to specific professional groups. Twitter's fast-paced nature lends itself to short, impactful messages and real-time engagement. TikTok's young, engaged audience requires a highly creative and engaging video format.

The strength of social media advertising lies in its ability to precisely target specific audience segments based on their interests, demographics, and online behavior. Sophisticated targeting options allow you to focus your ad spend on the users most likely to engage with your product or service, minimizing wasted ad spend. Moreover, social media platforms provide extensive analytical tools to monitor campaign performance and make data-driven adjustments. This allows you to continually optimize your campaigns, improving their effectiveness over time. However, the constantly evolving algorithms of social media platforms require continuous adaptation. What works today might not work tomorrow, necessitating ongoing attention and optimization. The cost of advertising on social media can also vary significantly depending on the platform, the level of competition, and the sophistication of your targeting.

Beyond Google Ads and social media advertising, numerous other paid advertising channels exist, each offering unique advantages depending on your specific needs. Programmatic advertising, for example, utilizes sophisticated algorithms to automate the buying and selling of ad inventory across multiple platforms, ensuring efficient delivery of your ads to the most relevant audience. This approach is particularly effective for reaching large audiences across diverse channels. However, it requires a robust understanding of programmatic technologies and a significant investment in specialized software and expertise.

Affiliate marketing, another prominent channel, involves partnering with other websites or influencers to promote your products or services. Affiliates earn a commission for each sale or lead generated through their marketing efforts, creating a mutually beneficial relationship. This approach can be highly effective for expanding your reach and driving sales, particularly through trusted sources within your niche. Careful selection of your affiliate partners is crucial to ensure the integrity of your brand and the effectiveness of your campaigns.

Native advertising involves seamlessly integrating paid ads into the existing content of a website or platform, making them less obtrusive and more engaging than traditional banner ads. This approach aims to enhance user experience by providing relevant content in a non-intrusive manner. However, creating compelling native ads that effectively blend into the existing content requires creative skill and a deep understanding of the platform's style and audience.

Email marketing, while often discussed in the context of organic reach, also employs paid advertising components. Paid email marketing can involve utilizing platforms that offer advanced email sending capabilities, targeting specific demographics or behaviors within your email list, and leveraging retargeting campaigns to reach prospects who have previously interacted with your website or brand. The strategic integration of paid advertising within your email campaigns can significantly boost your conversion rates.

Choosing the right paid advertising channels requires careful consideration of your business goals, target audience, budget, and available resources. A multi-channel approach, combining different channels to create a comprehensive marketing strategy, is often the most effective approach. For instance, a small business with a limited budget might start with Google Ads and Facebook advertising, focusing on highly targeted campaigns. A larger business with a significant marketing budget might utilize a multi-channel approach, incorporating programmatic advertising, affiliate marketing, and native advertising in addition to social media and search engine marketing.

Successful paid advertising campaigns are not simply about spending money; they are about strategically allocating resources to maximize ROI. This requires meticulous planning, precise targeting, compelling ad copy, and ongoing monitoring and optimization. Regularly analyzing your campaign performance data and making data-driven adjustments is crucial to achieving the desired results. This iterative approach allows you to continuously refine your campaigns, improving their effectiveness over time.

To illustrate successful paid advertising campaigns, let's consider several examples. A small e-commerce business specializing in handcrafted jewelry might use Instagram advertising to target a specific demographic interested in fashion and jewelry. By creating visually appealing ads showcasing their unique designs, they can drive traffic to their online store and increase sales. A B2B software company might use LinkedIn advertising to reach professionals in their target industry, using targeted ads that highlight the value proposition of their software. A local restaurant might utilize Google Ads to target customers searching for restaurants in their area, increasing their online visibility and attracting new customers. These examples showcase the diverse applications of paid advertising across various business sectors.

In conclusion, paid advertising offers a versatile and powerful toolkit for achieving your marketing objectives. However, navigating this complex landscape requires careful planning, strategic resource allocation, and continuous monitoring and optimization. By understanding the strengths and weaknesses of different channels and tailoring your approach to your specific business goals and target audience, you can harness the power of paid advertising to drive significant growth and success. The key is not simply to advertise, but to advertise effectively, leveraging data-driven insights to optimize your campaigns and maximize your return on investment.

Creating Effective Paid Advertising Campaigns

Creating effective paid advertising campaigns requires a multifaceted approach, extending far beyond simply allocating a budget and launching ads. It's a strategic process demanding careful planning, meticulous execution, and constant optimization. This involves understanding your target audience, selecting the appropriate channels, crafting compelling ad copy, and implementing effective bidding strategies. Ignoring any of these components can significantly diminish your return on investment (ROI).

Let's begin with keyword research, the cornerstone of successful search engine advertising (SEA) campaigns like those on Google Ads. While seemingly straightforward, identifying the right keywords requires a deeper understanding than just brainstorming relevant terms. Effective keyword research involves utilizing various tools and techniques to uncover high-volume, low-competition keywords that align precisely with your target audience's search intent. Tools like Google Keyword Planner, Ahrefs, SEMrush, and Moz Keyword Explorer provide valuable insights into search volume, competition, and keyword difficulty. Beyond simply identifying keywords, understanding long-tail keywords – longer, more specific phrases – is crucial. These phrases often have lower competition but higher conversion rates because they indicate a stronger purchase intent. For example, instead of the broad keyword "shoes," a more effective long-tail keyword might be "women's size 8 running shoes for flat feet."

Once you've identified your target keywords, the next step is crafting compelling ad copy. Your ad copy is your first and potentially only impression on a potential customer, so it needs to be concise, persuasive, and highly relevant to the keyword and search intent. A well-written ad copy should clearly communicate the value proposition of your product or service, highlighting key benefits and addressing the user's needs. It should also include a strong call to action (CTA), encouraging users to click through to your website or landing page. A/B testing different ad copy variations is crucial for optimizing your campaign's performance. This involves creating multiple versions of your ad copy with slight variations in headline, description, and CTA, and then tracking their performance to identify the most effective version.

Targeting is the art of directing your ads to the most receptive audience. This involves using various targeting options offered by different advertising platforms to ensure your ads reach only those most likely to be interested in your product or service. Google Ads, for instance, provides extensive targeting options based on demographics, location, interests, search history, and even device type. Social media platforms like Facebook and Instagram offer similar targeting options, allowing you to target users based on their interests, demographics, behavior, and even connections. Precise targeting is essential for maximizing your ROI and minimizing wasted ad spend. The more precisely you target your audience, the higher the likelihood of engagement and conversions.

Bidding strategies are equally crucial. Different bidding strategies are available, each with its own strengths and weaknesses. Cost-per-click (CPC) bidding is the most common approach, where you pay only when a user clicks on your ad. However, you can also use other bidding strategies, such as cost-per-thousand impressions (CPM) or cost-per-acquisition (CPA), depending on your campaign goals. Understanding the nuances of different bidding strategies and selecting the one that best aligns with your objectives is paramount. Automated bidding strategies offered by many platforms can help optimize your bids based on performance data, but manual adjustments are often necessary for fine-tuning.

Creating effective ad creatives is just as crucial as the other elements discussed. The visual aspects of your ads, including images, videos, and animations, can significantly impact their effectiveness. High-quality visuals that are engaging and relevant to your product or service are essential for capturing attention and driving clicks. For example, a video ad showcasing the benefits of a product is often more engaging than a static image. Similarly, using high-resolution images that are visually appealing can significantly improve your click-through rate (CTR). Experimentation with different creative styles and formats is essential for finding what resonates best with your target audience. A/B testing different creatives, just as with ad copy, is vital for continuous improvement.

Measuring and optimizing your campaigns is an ongoing process. Regularly analyzing campaign performance data is crucial for identifying what's working and what's not. Key metrics to track include CTR, conversion rate, cost per conversion, ROI, and return on ad spend (ROAS). Monitoring these metrics allows you to identify areas for improvement and make data-driven adjustments to optimize your campaigns. This iterative process of monitoring, analyzing, and optimizing is essential for maximizing your ROI and achieving your campaign goals. This often involves making changes to keywords, ad copy, targeting, and bidding strategies based on the performance data collected. Tools provided by advertising platforms offer dashboards to visualize and analyze this data, making the optimization process more efficient.

To illustrate these concepts with real-world examples, consider a small business selling artisanal coffee beans. Their effective paid advertising campaign would likely incorporate the following: keyword research focusing on terms like "organic coffee beans," "specialty coffee," and "fair-trade coffee," along with long-tail keywords like "best organic coffee beans for espresso." Their ad copy would emphasize the unique characteristics of their beans and highlight the ethical sourcing and quality roasting processes. Targeting would focus on coffee lovers, individuals with specific dietary preferences, and those interested in sustainable products, using demographic, interest, and behavioral targeting options on platforms like Facebook and Instagram. Their bidding strategy would focus on maximizing conversions, utilizing CPA bidding to optimize spending. Their ad creatives would feature high-quality images and videos showcasing the beans and the roasting process, perhaps even featuring customer testimonials. Regular monitoring of key metrics would allow them to continually refine their campaign, adjusting keywords, copy, targeting, and bidding strategies to maximize ROI.

Another example: a technology company launching a new software product. Their keyword research might include terms like "project management software," "collaboration tools," and specific software features. Their ad copy would highlight the software's unique features and benefits, addressing the pain points of their target audience (e.g., improved productivity, better team collaboration). Targeting would focus on professionals in relevant industries, leveraging LinkedIn advertising to reach decision-makers. Their bidding strategy would likely focus on lead generation, using CPA bidding to optimize for acquiring high-quality leads. Their ad creatives might use professional graphics and testimonials from satisfied users. Again, continuous monitoring and optimization would be essential for success.

In conclusion, creating highly effective paid advertising campaigns is a continuous cycle of planning, execution, monitoring, and optimization. By systematically addressing each stage—keyword research, ad copywriting, targeting, bidding strategies, ad creatives, and performance monitoring —businesses can leverage paid advertising to achieve significant growth. Remember that success isn't solely about spending more; it's about spending smarter, using data-driven insights to optimize your campaigns and maximize your return on investment. The key is to approach paid advertising as a strategic investment, not just an expense.

Tracking Measuring and Optimizing Paid Advertising Campaigns

Tracking, measuring, and optimizing your paid advertising campaigns is not a one-time event; it's an ongoing process demanding consistent attention and iterative refinement. Think of it as a continuous feedback loop, where data informs decisions, leading to improved performance. Without this crucial step, your advertising spend becomes a gamble, rather than a strategic investment.

The first critical step is identifying the key performance indicators (KPIs) relevant to your campaign objectives. While every campaign is unique, some universal metrics provide valuable insights regardless of your specific goals. Let's delve into some of the most important metrics:

Click-Through Rate (CTR): This metric measures the percentage of users who click on your ad after seeing it. A high CTR suggests your ad copy and visuals are compelling and relevant to your target audience. Low CTRs, however, signal potential problems with your ad's message, targeting, or even its placement. Analyzing CTRs by different ad variations or target groups can unveil where improvements are needed. For instance, if a particular demographic has a consistently low CTR, it may indicate a need to refine your targeting or messaging to better resonate with that group. Always compare CTR against industry benchmarks to gauge your performance accurately.

Conversion Rate: This metric indicates the percentage of users who complete a desired action after clicking on your ad. This action could be anything from making a purchase, filling out a form, signing up for a newsletter, or downloading a resource. A high conversion rate signifies that your landing page is effective at converting clicks into desired actions. A low conversion rate, on the other hand, suggests that your landing page may need improvement in terms of design, messaging, or call-to-action. Optimizing the user experience on the landing page is crucial to improving conversion rates. This could involve streamlining the checkout process, reducing distractions, or improving the clarity of your messaging.

Cost Per Acquisition (CPA): CPA measures the average cost of acquiring a customer or achieving a specific conversion. This metric is essential for evaluating the efficiency of your campaign in terms of return on investment (ROI). A low CPA indicates that you are efficiently acquiring customers or achieving conversions. Conversely, a high CPA suggests that you need to optimize your campaign to reduce costs without sacrificing conversions. Analyzing your CPA across different channels, ad sets, or keywords can highlight areas for cost optimization. For instance, if a particular keyword consistently yields a high CPA, it may be necessary to adjust your bidding strategy or even remove the keyword from your campaign.

Return on Ad Spend (ROAS): ROAS represents the revenue generated for every dollar spent on advertising. It's a crucial metric for evaluating the overall profitability of your campaigns. A high ROAS signifies that your campaigns are generating a significant return on investment, while a low ROAS indicates that your campaigns are not profitable and require optimization. Tracking ROAS is essential for understanding the long-term impact of your advertising efforts and justifying continued investment. A decline in ROAS could prompt investigation into several factors, including changes in market conditions, audience behaviour, or campaign performance.

Return on Investment (ROI): While ROAS specifically focuses on advertising revenue, ROI takes a broader view of profitability, considering all costs associated with your business's revenue generation. This metric provides a comprehensive perspective on the effectiveness of your advertising investment within the bigger picture of your business.

Beyond these core metrics, other important indicators include:

Impression Share: The percentage of times your ad was shown compared to the total number of times it could have been shown. A low impression share suggests a need to adjust your bidding strategy or improve your ad's quality score.

Average Position: Indicates the average position your ad holds on the search results page or within a social media feed. A higher average position generally implies better visibility and potentially higher CTR.

Quality Score: A measure of how relevant and engaging your ads are, impacting your ad's visibility and cost. Google Ads, for example, uses this metric to influence your ad ranking and cost-per-click.

To effectively utilize these metrics, you need robust tracking and analytical tools. Most major advertising platforms provide comprehensive dashboards with detailed reports on campaign performance. Google Ads, Facebook Ads Manager, and LinkedIn Campaign Manager are just a few examples. These platforms offer granular data allowing you to analyze performance across various dimensions, such as:

Device: How your ads perform on different devices (desktop, mobile, tablet) to inform ad creatives and targeting strategies.

Location: Geographic areas where your ads are most or least effective, providing insights into audience concentration and campaign targeting efficiency.

Time of Day: Identifying peak performance times can optimize ad scheduling for maximum reach and conversions.

Keywords: Which keywords generate the most clicks, conversions, and positive ROAS, assisting with keyword optimization.

Ad Creatives: Comparing the performance of different ad creatives (images, videos, text) to identify what resonates most effectively with your audience.

Once you've gathered this data, the next step involves translating the insights into actionable strategies. This is where data-driven decision-making plays a crucial role.

Let's illustrate with some examples:

Suppose your CTR is low but your impression share is high. This indicates that while your ads are being shown frequently, they aren't engaging your target audience. This necessitates re-evaluating your ad copy, creatives, or targeting parameters. Perhaps your messaging isn't compelling enough, or your visuals aren't capturing attention. Testing alternative ad copies, images, or videos can help you identify the most effective combination.

If your conversion rate is low despite a high CTR, the problem lies with your landing page. A weak landing page might be confusing, poorly designed, or not effectively leading users toward your desired conversion goal. Optimizations might involve A/B testing different landing page layouts, streamlining the user journey, or improving the clarity of your call-to-action.

A high CPA suggests your campaign is inefficient. Possible solutions include: refining your targeting to reach a more qualified audience, adjusting your bidding strategy to optimize for conversions, experimenting with different ad formats to reduce costs, or improving your ad quality score to reduce your cost-per-click.

The process of analyzing campaign data, making adjustments, and monitoring the results is continuous. It's an iterative cycle of optimization, where each iteration builds upon the previous one, leading to progressively improved campaign performance. Regularly reviewing your data (daily or weekly, depending on campaign scale) ensures you identify problems early and quickly implement corrective measures, maximizing your return on ad spend. Don't wait for significant losses to arise; make monitoring and optimization a key element of your advertising strategy. Consistent monitoring and optimization are integral to ensuring that your paid advertising investment is delivering optimal results.

Budget Allocation and Campaign Management

Budget allocation and campaign management are critical components of a successful paid advertising strategy. Throwing money at ads without a clear plan is akin to throwing darts blindfolded – you might get lucky, but it's far from a guaranteed win. A well-defined budget allocation strategy, coupled with meticulous campaign management, transforms paid advertising from a gamble into a strategic investment, maximizing your return on investment (ROI).

The first step is to define your overall marketing budget and allocate a portion specifically to paid advertising. This allocation should be directly tied to your business objectives. Are you aiming for rapid brand awareness, driving immediate sales, or generating leads? Your objectives will heavily influence how you distribute your budget across different channels and campaigns. For example, a company launching a new product might dedicate a larger portion of its budget to brand awareness campaigns on platforms like Instagram or YouTube, while an established business focusing on lead generation might prioritize Google Ads or LinkedIn.

Setting realistic and attainable budget goals is crucial. Don't overextend yourself. It's far better to start with a smaller, manageable budget and gradually increase it as you learn what works best and refine your strategies. Many businesses find a phased approach helpful – initiating with a smaller-scale campaign to test different ad creatives, target audiences, and bidding strategies before scaling up based on initial performance.

Once you have a budget, you need a robust system to track your expenses. This goes beyond simply monitoring the amount spent on each platform. You should track expenses across specific campaigns, ad sets, keywords, and even individual ad creatives. This granular level of tracking provides insights into what's working and what's not, informing future budget decisions. Using spreadsheet software, dedicated marketing analytics dashboards, or integrated campaign management tools allows for efficient expense tracking and data analysis. Many modern marketing platforms provide integrated reporting tools, streamlining the tracking process.

Campaign management involves the day-to-day optimization of your paid advertising efforts. This is a continuous process, not a one-off task. Regular monitoring, analysis, and adjustment of your campaigns are crucial for optimal performance. This includes:

Keyword Management (for search advertising):
Continuously review your keyword performance. Are certain keywords driving high conversions and a strong ROAS? Are others underperforming and costing you money? Pause or remove ineffective keywords and allocate more budget to high-performing ones. Regularly identify new relevant keywords to expand your reach. Utilize keyword research tools to expand your keyword base strategically.

A/B Testing: A/B testing involves creating multiple versions of your ads (different headlines, images, calls to action) and running them simultaneously to determine which performs best. This allows you to identify the most effective creatives and optimize your campaigns for maximum impact. Consistent A/B testing across your ads, landing pages, and even email sequences helps refine your marketing materials for optimal response rates.

Audience Targeting: Continuously refine your audience targeting. Begin with broad targeting and then narrow it down based on performance data. For example, if you are targeting a specific age group or geographic location and observing low engagement, you may need to adjust your targeting parameters to a more relevant segment of your market.

Bidding Strategy: Regularly review and adjust your bidding strategy. Do you want to prioritize impressions, clicks, conversions, or a combination of these? Consider different bidding strategies offered by each platform (e.g., automated bidding vs. manual bidding) to optimize your budget allocation. Automated bidding can be beneficial for scaling campaigns, while manual bidding provides more precise control, particularly helpful during the initial stages of campaign launch.

Landing Page Optimization: Your landing page is crucial for converting clicks into actions. Ensure your landing pages are optimized for conversions, with clear calls to action, relevant messaging, and a streamlined user experience. A/B test different landing page variations to identify the most effective design and messaging to maximize conversion rates. A strong landing page creates a seamless transition between your ad and the next desired action from the customer.

A successful budget allocation strategy involves a clear understanding of your return on ad spend (ROAS) for each campaign. If one campaign isn't performing well, don't be afraid to reallocate budget to those that are delivering better results. Regularly analyze your ROAS across different campaigns, platforms, and keywords to inform your budget allocation decisions. A comprehensive understanding of

ROAS across the various dimensions of your campaign gives you the data you need to dynamically adjust your budget for optimal performance.

Let's illustrate this with a concrete example: Imagine a small e-commerce business selling handmade jewelry. Their initial budget is $1000 per month. They decide to allocate $500 to Facebook Ads, $300 to Instagram Ads, and $200 to Google Ads. After the first month, they analyze their results. They discover that Facebook Ads generated a ROAS of 3:1 (meaning they made $1500 in revenue for every $500 spent), Instagram Ads generated a ROAS of 1.5:1 ($450 profit from $300 spent), and Google Ads had a poor ROAS of 0.8:1 (a $160 loss from $200 spent). Based on this data, for the second month, they would likely increase their Facebook Ads budget significantly, potentially reducing the Instagram Ads budget slightly, and drastically reducing or eliminating the Google Ads budget altogether. They may also explore a different platform or a different strategy for Google Ads based on what they've learned. This iterative approach allows them to optimize their budget allocation for maximal returns.

Another crucial aspect of campaign management is reporting. Regularly generate reports that summarize your campaign performance, highlighting key metrics such as CTR, conversion rate, CPA, and ROAS. These reports should be shared with relevant stakeholders to provide transparency and demonstrate the effectiveness of your paid advertising strategy. Clear and concise reports facilitate easier understanding of the results achieved and their impact on the overall business performance. They can also help justify continued investment in paid advertising efforts by demonstrating a strong return on investment.

Ultimately, successful budget allocation and campaign management are iterative processes that demand continuous monitoring, analysis, and adaptation. It's a cycle of learning, refining, and optimizing to maximize your results. By meticulously tracking your spending, analyzing your data, and making data-driven decisions, you can transform your paid advertising efforts from a potentially costly exercise into a powerful engine for business growth. The key is continuous monitoring and improvement, adapting to changes in market trends, and making informed adjustments based on the data you collect. This ensures that your budget is allocated efficiently and that your campaigns are continuously optimized for maximum return. Remember, consistent effort in monitoring, analyzing, and refining your campaigns is crucial for long-term success.

Case Studies RealWorld Examples of Successful Paid Advertising

Let's delve into the practical application of paid advertising strategies through real-world examples. These case studies demonstrate how different businesses, across diverse industries, have effectively utilized paid advertising to achieve their specific marketing objectives. Analyzing these successes and challenges offers valuable insights into best practices and potential pitfalls.

Our first case study features "GreenThumb Gardens," a small, family-owned business specializing in organic gardening supplies. Their primary goal was to increase brand awareness and drive traffic to their online store. Initially, GreenThumb Gardens allocated a modest budget of $500 per month to Google Ads. Their strategy focused on long-tail keywords related to organic gardening, such as "organic vegetable seeds near me," "best organic soil for tomatoes," and "how to start an organic herb garden." They created concise, informative ad copy highlighting the quality and sustainability of their products, emphasizing their commitment to environmentally friendly practices. Crucially, their landing page was optimized for conversions, featuring high-quality product images, detailed descriptions, and a clear call-to-action.

The results were impressive. Within three months, GreenThumb Gardens saw a significant increase in website traffic, a 25% rise in online sales, and a marked improvement in brand visibility. Their return on ad spend (ROAS) exceeded 4:1, demonstrating the effectiveness of their targeted keyword strategy and optimized landing page. A key lesson learned was the importance of consistently monitoring keyword performance and adjusting bids based on real-time data. Keywords that underperformed were quickly paused, allowing for a more efficient allocation of their advertising budget. They also incorporated A/B testing on their ad copy and landing page, iteratively refining their approach to maximize conversion rates.

Next, let's consider "TechSolutions," a rapidly growing software development company aiming to generate leads for their new project management software. Their strategy involved a multi-channel approach, utilizing LinkedIn Ads and Google Ads in tandem. On LinkedIn, they targeted professionals in project management roles, showcasing the software's key features and benefits through visually appealing video ads. Their Google Ads campaign focused on broader keywords, such as "project management software," "best project management tools," and "agile project management." To capture leads, they used lead generation forms directly integrated into their ads, requesting contact information from interested users.

TechSolutions meticulously tracked their results, monitoring key metrics such as click-through rates (CTR), cost-per-click (CPC), conversion rates, and cost-per-lead (CPL). Their LinkedIn campaign proved particularly successful, generating a high number of qualified leads with a relatively low CPL. However, their Google Ads campaign yielded a lower conversion rate and higher CPL. Analyzing this discrepancy, TechSolutions realized their Google Ads targeting was too broad, attracting individuals not directly involved in project management. They refined their Google Ads campaign by implementing more specific targeting parameters, focusing on keywords more closely related to the software's core functionalities and its target audience. This adjustment improved their campaign's performance significantly. Through continuous optimization and a multi-channel approach, TechSolutions effectively generated a steady flow of qualified leads, validating the importance of data-driven adjustments.

Our third case study focuses on "CozyCottage Candles," a small business selling handcrafted candles. Their initial paid advertising strategy centered around Instagram Ads, utilizing high-quality product images and engaging video content. Their target audience was defined by demographics and interests, focusing on individuals who follow accounts related to home décor, relaxation, and self-care. They ran several A/B tests on their ad creatives, experimenting with different visuals and copy to determine which resonated most effectively with their target audience. The results were promising, but initially, their ROAS was modest.

Analyzing the data, CozyCottage Candles realized that their landing page was not optimized for conversions. The checkout process was cumbersome, and the call-to-action was unclear. After redesigning their landing page with a more user-friendly interface and a stronger call-to-action, their conversion rate drastically improved, leading to a substantial increase in their ROAS. This highlights the critical role of landing page optimization in maximizing the effectiveness of paid advertising campaigns. It's not enough to simply drive traffic to your website; you must ensure that your website effectively converts visitors into customers.

In contrast to the previous examples, let's examine a scenario where paid advertising didn't initially yield expected results. "Artisan Bakers," a local bakery with a strong following, decided to run a Facebook Ads campaign to promote a new line of gourmet cookies. Their initial campaign used broad targeting and generic ad copy. Despite a significant budget allocation, the campaign underperformed. The click-through rate was low, and the conversion rate was even lower.

Upon reviewing the campaign's performance, Artisan Bakers realized several key shortcomings. Firstly, their targeting was too broad, reaching individuals who weren't likely interested in gourmet cookies. Secondly, their ad copy lacked compelling messaging and didn't effectively convey the unique selling points of their cookies. Finally, their landing page lacked a clear call-to-action. After adjusting their targeting to focus on local demographics with an interest in desserts and baking, crafting compelling ad copy highlighting the unique flavors and ingredients, and optimizing their landing page for conversions, Artisan Bakers experienced a remarkable turnaround. The revised campaign achieved a substantially higher ROAS, demonstrating the critical importance of precise targeting, persuasive messaging, and optimized landing pages. This case study underscores the necessity of iterative refinement and the willingness to adapt one's strategy in light of performance data.

These case studies demonstrate the diverse ways paid advertising can be leveraged to achieve different marketing goals. Success hinges on meticulous planning, ongoing optimization, and a deep understanding of your target audience. Remember, paid advertising is not a one-size-fits-all solution. The optimal strategy will vary based on your specific business goals, industry, target audience, and budget. The common thread among these successful campaigns is the commitment to continuous monitoring, analysis, and adaptation. By consistently analyzing performance data and making data-driven decisions, businesses can maximize their return on investment and achieve sustainable growth. It's not merely about spending money on ads; it's about strategically investing in a measurable and refined approach that delivers results. The key takeaway from these diverse examples is the power of data-driven decision-making and iterative improvement in achieving effective paid advertising campaigns. By understanding the nuances of each platform, refining targeting strategies, and constantly analyzing results, businesses can unlock the true potential of paid advertising and drive significant business growth.